Transboundary Waters, Infrastructure Development and Public Private Partnership

International Water Law

Editor-in-Chief

Salman M. A. Salman (*IWRA*)

Associate Editors

Laurence Boisson de Chazournes (*University of Geneva*)
Lilian del Castillo-Laborde (*University of Buenos Aires*)
Gabriel Eckstein (*Texas A&M University*)
Makane Moïse Mbengue (*University of Geneva*)
Alistair Rieu-Clarke (*Northumbria University*)
Kishor Uprety (*International Lawyer and Researcher*)

Volumes published in this Brill Research Perspectives title are listed at *brill.com/rpwl*

Transboundary Waters, Infrastructure Development and Public Private Partnership

Through the Prism of the Nam Thuen 2 and Xayaburi Hydropower Projects

By

Richard Kyle Paisley
Riley T. Denoon
Theressa Etmanski
Patrick Weiler

BRILL

LEIDEN | BOSTON

Originally published as Volume 2(4) 2017, in *International Water Law*, DOI 10.1163/23529369-12340008.

Library of Congress Control Number: 2017953961

Typeface for the Latin, Greek, and Cyrillic scripts: "Brill". See and download: brill.com/brill-typeface.

ISBN 978-90-04-35975-8 (paperback)
ISBN 978-90-04-35976-5 (e-book)

Copyright 2017 by Richard Kyle Paisley, Riley T. Denoon, Theressa Etmanski, Patrick Weiler. Published by Koninklijke Brill NV, Leiden, The Netherlands.
Koninklijke Brill NV incorporates the imprints Brill, Brill Hes & De Graaf, Brill Nijhoff, Brill Rodopi, Brill Sense and Hotei Publishing.
Koninklijke Brill NV reserves the right to protect the publication against unauthorized use and to authorize dissemination by means of offprints, legitimate photocopies, microform editions, reprints, translations, and secondary information sources, such as abstracting and indexing services including databases. Requests for commercial re-use, use of parts of the publication, and/or translations must be addressed to Koninklijke Brill NV.

This book is printed on acid-free paper and produced in a sustainable manner.

Contents

Transboundary Waters, Infrastructure Development and Public Private Partnership
Through the Prism of the Nam Thuen 2 and Xayaburi Hydropower Projects   1

    Abstract   1
    Keywords   2
    Introduction   2
  A   Public-Private Partnerships   4
      I   *What is a Public-Private Partnership?*   4
      II   *Types of Public-Private Partnerships*   5
      III   *Why do PPPs Matter?*   6
  B   International Watercourses Law and PPPs   9
      I   *PPPs on International Watercourses and the Law of International Watercourses*   10
          (a)   State Actors   10
      II   *International Treaties*   11
          (a)   The UN Convention on the Law of the Non-navigational Uses of International Watercourses   12
      III   *Customary International Law*   14
      IV   *Application to the Nam Theun 2 Project*   15
  C   The Governance of PPPs through 'Policies' of Multilateral Development Banks   16
      I   *Streams of International Governance of PPPs through the World Bank Group*   16
          (a)   The World Bank's 'Safeguard' Polices   17
          (b)   Other Safeguard Policies   19
          (c)   Substantive Obligations   20
              (i)   Notification   20
              (ii)   No Harm   22
      II   *Other Multilateral Development Banks*   22
      III   *The International Finance Corporation's Performance Standards*   23
      IV   *China and Chinese Development*   25
          (a)   The Asian Infrastructure Investment Bank   26
  D   The Mekong River Basin, the 1995 Mekong Agreement and the Nam Theun 2 Hydropower Project   27
      I   *NT2 is Located in Lao PDR in the Mekong River Basin*   28

	II	*1995 Agreement on the Cooperation for the Sustainable Development of the Mekong River Basin* 28
		(a) Structure of the MRC 30
		(b) Financing 32
		(c) Data and Information Exchange 33
		(d) Flexibility 33
		(e) Dispute Resolution 34
		(f) Key Initiatives Launched Since the 1995 Mekong Agreement 35
	III	*The Nam Theun 2 Project* 38
		(a) Context 38
		(b) NT2 Specifications 40
		(c) History 41
		(d) Financing and Equity 41
		(e) Impacts 42
		(f) Significance 43
E	Contractual Structure 44	
	I	*PPP Contractual Structure* 45
	II	*Key Elements* 47
	III	*The Nam Theun 2 Hydropower Project* 48
F	Project Cost and Financing/Risk Mitigation 49	
	I	*Project Cost* 50
	II	*Project Capital Structure* 51
	III	*Mitigating Risks* 51
	IV	*Political Risk Guarantees* 52
G	Xayaburi Project 57	
H	Concluding Remarks 62	

List of References 65

Transboundary Waters, Infrastructure Development and Public Private Partnership

Through the Prism of the Nam Thuen 2 and Xayaburi Hydropower Projects

    Richard Paisley
M.Sc, J.D., LL.M., International Waters Governance Initiative, University of British Columbia, Canada
    rpaisley@mail.ubc.ca

    Riley Denoon
J.D., LL.M., J.S.D. Candidate, University of the Pacific, McGeorge School of Law, United States
    rdenoon@gmail.com

    Theressa Etmanski
J.D., M.A., International Waters Governance Initiative, University of British Columbia, Canada
    theressa.etmanski@gmail.com

    Patrick Weiler
J.D., International Waters Governance Initiative, University of British Columbia, Canada
    patrickbsweiler@gmail.com

Abstract

Governments increasingly look to the private sector for the financing, design, construction, and operation of infrastructure projects, and as a result, public-private partnerships (PPPs) have emerged as a valuable source for investment funds and expertise. PPPs involving new uses of transboundary waters require giving particular attention to the huge potential for environmental and social impacts. This monograph examines what PPPs are and how they, and environmental and social 'safeguards,' function in a transboundary waters context and with each other. This examination is undertaken through the prism of the Nam Theun 2 and Xayaburi hydroelectric power projects in Lao PDR. This monograph discusses and draws some important lessons from these PPPs contractual arrangements, costs, financing, and risk mitigation, for PPPs to be contemplated in other transboundary waters contexts.

Keywords

infrastructure – Nam Theun 2 – public-private partnerships – transboundary watercourses – Xayaburi

Introduction

Through the examples of the Nam Theun 2 (NT2) and Xayaburi hydroelectric power projects in Laos PDR, this monograph provides a subject overview of public-private partnerships (PPPs) for infrastructure development on transboundary international waters and the applicable law of transboundary watercourses. It takes into account recent scholarship and provides a discussion of some of the most important publications on the subject.

Increasing use of PPP financing models are a critical tool to address the ever-widening global infrastructure gap. In the first half of 2016 alone, US$29.5 billion was invested in infrastructure projects with private sector participation, including US$9.3 billion in renewable energy projects (which include hydropower).[1] This manuscript will examine the implications of the increased use of this tool on projects associated with transboundary watercourses.

Part A provides an overarching explanation of PPPs, including the different contractual structures PPPs may take, and highlights the relevance of PPPs for the development of infrastructure and poverty reduction measures in emerging and developing economies. It also reviews some common advantages and identifies potential disadvantages of PPPs as a funding model. Part B outlines relevant international watercourses law at play in the context of the NT2 project. It explains public international law's application to the relevant actors involved in PPPs; summarizes applicable international treaties, including the United Nations Convention on the Law of Non-navigational Uses of International Watercourses; and reviews other relevant sources of the law of international watercourses developed over time.

---

1   'Private Participation in Infrastructure Database (PPIDB)—Half Year Update (January–June 2016), *The World Bank Group* (2016), p. 1, https://ppi.worldbank.org/~/media/GIAWB/PPI/Documents/Global-Notes/H1–2016-Global-Update.pdf, accessed January 13, 2017.

In Part C, the governance of PPPs is further discussed through a review of the policies of multilateral development banks, including the World Bank[2] safeguard policies, which regulate obligations between riparian neighbours with respect to the potential shared impacts of infrastructure development along international waterways. This section also traces the emerging policies of other multilateral development banks, such as the new Asian Infrastructure Development Bank, and states, such as China.

Part D situates NT2 within the geographical context of the Mekong River Basin. The shared use of this international watercourse is governed in part by the 1995 Mekong Agreement, which creates an institutional framework for cooperation among states. This section provides an overview of this governance structure, including how administrative costs are financed, how data and information are exchanged, and how disputes are resolved. It also presents a summary of key initiatives launched since the 1995 Mekong Agreement came into existence and discusses the development, history and implementation of the NT2. The section concludes by summarizing the impacts and significance of the NT2, addressing both effects on the Lao PDR economy and capacity development, as well as the policies and practice of the World Bank.

Part E addresses the relevant contractual forms and terms associated with a PPP and provides a brief overview of the contractual makeup of NT2. Part F provides an overview of the development of the financing agreement and the resulting capital structure that was concluded by Lao PDR, the World Bank, and other contributing investors. It discusses how the due diligence risk mitigation work of the World Bank and other international financial institutions played a pivotal role in attracting partners in the private sector and other financial backers to the project. The section concludes with a summary of the financial plan that was ultimately reached to develop and implement NT2.

---

2   As can be discerned from this overview, the World Bank plays a prominent role in this monograph's discussion of public-private partnerships (PPPs) through the prism of NT2. For the purposes of this monograph the term 'World Bank' or 'the Bank' will be used to refer to the two following member entities of the World Bank Group: International Bank for Reconstruction and Development (IBRD) and the International Development Association (IDA). The International Finance Corporation (IFC) will be referred to, mostly, separately, even though the IFC is also a member of the World Bank Group. However, the term 'World Bank Group' will also be used in the monograph to refer to these three entities. It should be added in the context that the term 'World Bank Group' also includes two more entities: the Multilateral Investment Guarantee Agency (MIGA) and the International Centre for Settlement of Investment Disputes (ICSID). For more on the World Bank Group and these five entities see http://www.brettonwoodsproject.org/2005/08/art-320854/

Part G introduces critical reviews and compares NT2 and another large PPP infrastructure project in Lao PDR waterways, the Xayaburi hydroelectric power project (Xayaburi). Contrasts that are noted include the varying impact of Xayaburi by, and on, the Mekong River Commission, varying financing arrangements and domestic and transboundary social and environmental concerns.

Part H, the conclusion, reviews some of the key lessons learned through the NT2's PPP model and identifies conditions for success of future PPP projects in a similar context. This monograph aims to provide a starting point for research on these subjects. The attached bibliography provides a guide for further exploration into these topics.

A   Public-Private Partnerships

This section provides a general explanation of PPPs, including the different structures PPPs may take, and highlights the relevance of PPPs for the development of infrastructure and poverty reduction in emerging and developing economies. It also reviews some common advantages of PPPs as a funding model, while also identifying potential disadvantages.

I   *What is a Public-Private Partnership?*

The expression 'public-private partnership' refers to a relationship between some form of public entity and a private one wherein the latter engages in activities on behalf of the former. Beyond this, there is no standard definition. For our purposes, the World Bank provides a workable definition of a PPP as a formal contractual relationship:

> A long-term contract between a private party and a government entity, for providing a public asset or service, in which the private party bears significant risk and management responsibility, and remuneration is linked to performance.[3]

---

3   'Public-Private Partnerships Reference Guide,' v. 2.0, *World Bank Group* (2014), p. 14, http://wwwwds.worldbank.org/external/default/WDSContentServer/WDSP/IB/2014/09/08/000442464_20140908133431/Rendered/PDF/903840PPP0Refe0Box385311B000PUBLIC0.pdf, accessed June 22, 2016.

TRANSBOUNDARY WATERS, INFRASTRUCTURE DEVELOPMENT 5

Even within this definition there are myriad uses and terms. For the purposes of this work we rely on the above definitions of a PPP. In particular, we discuss PPPs involving large-scale hydroelectric projects (HEP) on international watercourses.

II   Types of Public-Private Partnerships

The functions that private parties under an infrastructure PPP contractual structure are responsible for vary from project to project and depend upon the asset or service involved. Some typical responsibilities of a private party under a PPP are:

- Design or engineering to bring a project from initial concept to construction-ready specifications
- Build or rehabilitate a new or existing asset
- Finance all or part of the necessary capital expenditure
- Maintain the asset to a specified standard over the life of the contract
- Operate the asset or service, which can vary widely depending on the nature of the underlying asset and associated service[4]

Figure 1 sets out some common terms used to describe different structures for allocating responsibilities and risks in PPP projects.[5]

---

[4] For example, the private party could be responsible for operating the asset and providing the service directly to the user or a government off-taker, or, the private party could be responsible for providing support services to a government agency that provides the service to the ultimate users. See ibid., pp. 18–19. 'The options available for delivery of public services range from direct provision by a ministry or government department to outright privatization, where the government transfers all responsibilities, risks and rewards for service delivery to the private sector.' 'Guidebook on Promoting Good Governance in Public-Private Partnerships,' *United Nations Economic Commission for Europe* (2008), p. 3, http://www.unece.org/fileadmin/DAM/ceci/publications/ppp.pdf, accessed June 22, 2016.

[5] 'Guidebook on Promoting Good Governance in Public-Private Partnerships,' ibid., pp. 2–3.

> "Buy-Build-Operate (BBO): Transfer of a public asset to a private or quasi-public entity usually under contract that the assets are to be upgraded and operated for a specified period of time. Public control is exercised through the contract at the time of transfer.
>
> Build-Own-Operate (BOO): The private sector finances, builds, owns and operates a facility or service in perpetuity. The public constraints are stated in the original agreement and through on-going regulatory authority.
>
> Build-Own-Operate-Transfer (BOOT): A private entity receives a franchise to finance, design, build and operate a facility (and to charge user fees) for a specified period, after which ownership is transferred back to the public sector.
>
> Build-Operate-Transfer (BOT): The private sector designs, finances and constructs a new facility under a long-term Concession contract, and operates the facility during the term of the Concession after which ownership is transferred back to the public sector if not already transferred upon completion of the facility. In fact, such a form covers BOOT and BLOT with the sole difference being the ownership of the facility.
>
> Build-Lease-Operate-Transfer (BLOT): A private entity receives a franchise to finance, design, build and operate a leased facility (and to charge user fees) for the lease period, against payment of a rent.
>
> Design-Build-Finance-Operate (DBFO): The private sector designs, finances and constructs a new facility under a long-term lease, and operates the facility during the term of the lease. The private partner transfers the new facility to the public sector at the end of the lease term.
>
> Finance Only: A private entity, usually a financial services company, funds a project directly or uses various mechanisms such as a long-term lease or bond issue.
>
> Operation & Maintenance Contract (O & M): A private operator, under contract, operates a publicly owned asset for a specified term. Ownership of the asset remains with the public entity. (Many do not consider O&M's to be within the spectrum of PPPs and consider such contracts as service contracts.)
>
> Design-Build (DB): The private sector designs and builds infrastructure to meet public sector performance specifications, often for a fixed price, turnkey basis, so the risk of cost overruns is transferred to the private sector. (Many do not consider DB's to be within the spectrum of PPPs and consider such contracts as public works contracts.)
>
> Operation License: A private operator receives a license or rights to operate a public service, usually for a specified term. This is often used in IT projects."

FIGURE 1   *Text box of terms.*

III   *Why do PPPs Matter?*

The private sector and its powerful ability to mobilize capital in the search for profit provide an attractive engine to drive development on transboundary waters.[6] The involvement of the private sector on large-scale development

---

6   Many multilateral development banks have identified PPPs as an essential way to mobilize private capital and have set up specific resources to cater to facilitating PPPs and private sector involvement. See, for example, *European PPP Expertise Center (EPEC)*, European Investment Bank, http://www.eib.org/epec/index.htm, accessed September 13, 2016, and *The EPEC PPP Guide*, European Investment Bank, European PPP Expertise Center, http://www.eib.org/epec/g2g/index.htm, accessed September 13, 2016. The World Bank Group has established the *Public-Private-Partnership in Infrastructure Resource Centre (PPPIRC)*, World Bank

projects situated on transboundary waters hopefully allows for a better allocation of risk on these projects and for a more efficient delivery of public assets or services,[7] as well as a more streamlined allocation of expertise and innovation.[8]

Sovereign guarantees are often used to induce private investment, and are given by host governments to assure project lenders that the government will take certain actions or refrain from taking certain actions affecting the project. Governments offer sovereign guarantees to reduce investor risk and to create stability for the purpose of promoting project investment.[9]

In a joint statement issued November 2014, the heads of several multilateral development banks (MDBs) left no doubt as to the importance of PPPs to their future plans. Increasingly tapping into private equity through PPPs is touted as a panacea, forming part of a bundle of methods for addressing the infrastructure gap in emerging and developing economies, estimated at over US$1 trillion per annum.[10] To this end MDB's seek to mobilize ever larger amounts of private sector involvement and capital through regulatory reforms, legal frameworks, country databases, and financing instruments, including the creation of new asset classes of social and economic infrastructure[11] that would be attractive to private sector participation without the need for sovereign guarantees.[12]

Group, https://ppp.worldbank.org/public-private-partnership/, accessed September 13, 2016; 'PPP Knowledge Lab: MDBs' Collaboration Brings You the First-ever Comprehensive Online Resource for Public-Private Partnerships,' *World Bank Group* (January 25, 2016), http://www.worldbank.org/en/news/feature/2016/01/25/ppp-knowledge-lab, accessed September 13, 2016; *Public-Private Infrastructure Advisory Facility (PPIAF)*, World Bank Group, http://www.ppiaf.org, accessed September 13, 2016.

7 *Public-Private Partnerships, Overview*, World Bank Group, http://www.worldbank.org/en/topic/publicprivatepartnerships/overview, accessed June 22, 2016.

8 Samuel Colverson & Oshani Perera, 'Sustainable Development: Is There a Role for Public-Private Partnerships?,' *International Institute for Sustainable Development* (2011), p. 4, http://www.iisd.org/pdf/2011/sust_markets_PB_PPP.pdf, accessed June 24, 2016.

9 Tomas Magnusson, 'Sovereign Financial Guarantees,' Paper Prepared for *UNCTAD, UNDP, & UNITAR Workshop on Management of a Debt Office*, Tbilisi, Georgia (April 23, 1999).

10 'Statement by the Heads of the Multilateral Development Banks and the IMF on Infrastructure,' *World Bank Group* (November 13, 2014), http://www.worldbank.org/en/news/press-release/2014/11/13/statement-heads-multilateral-development-banks-imf-infrastructure, accessed June 22, 2016.

11 Nancy Alexander, *The Age of Megaprojects*, Project Syndicate (July 10, 2015), http://www.project-syndicate.org/commentary/g20-infrastructure-investment-by-nancy-alexander-2015–07, accessed June 22, 2016.

12 Statement by the Heads of the Multilateral Development Banks and the IMF on Infrastructure, supra note 10.

In 2014, it was estimated that the developing world was spending US$1 trillion on infrastructure, with only a fraction of that involving private actors.[13] The numbers for private investment and PPPs in developing countries was down in 2013, by US$36 billion, from 2012, but still amounted to US$150 billion.[14] As World Bank Group President Jim Yong Kim stated in October 2014:

> To fill [the investment] gap, we need to tap into the trillions of dollars held by institutional investors—most of which is sitting on the sidelines—and direct those assets into projects that will have great benefit for a range of developing countries ... it will take the commitment of all of us to help low- and middle-income countries bridge the massive infrastructure divide.[15]

The World Bank views PPPs as an avenue to address the Bank's twin goals: the elimination of extreme poverty and increasing shared prosperity. In 2015, then International Finance Corporation (IFC) executive vice president and chief executive officer, Jin Yong Cai, highlighted the role that he sees for PPPs in addressing the Bank's goals:

> Meeting these goals over the next 15 years will require trillions of dollars a year. It will require the world to unleash the power of market economies—which are most effective when they are fair, transparent, and inclusive. It's imperative for the public and private sectors to play their respective roles in this effort.[16]

It is worth noting that the views expressed by the World Bank Group's leadership in regard to the role of the public sector is not without criticism. The 'Washington Consensus,' at least in its neoliberal form, has become quite

---

13   Jim Yong Kim, 'Tackling the Most Difficult Problems: Infrastructure, Ebola and Climate Change,' *World Bank Group* (October 10, 2014), http://www.worldbank.org/en/news/speech/2014/10/10/speech-world-bank-group-president-jim-yong-kim-tackling-difficult-problems-infrastructure-ebola-climate-change, accessed June 22, 2016.
14   Ibid.
15   Ibid.
16   Jin-Yong Cai, 'A Letter from IFC executive vice president and chief executive officer Jin-Yong Cai,' *International Finance Corporation, World Bank Group* (2015), http://www.ifc.org/wps/wcm/connect/corp_ext_content/ifc_external_corporate_site/annual+report+2015/2015+online+report/leadership+perspectives/ar15_jyc+letter, accessed June 22, 2016.

controversial.[17] The role of the private sphere in providing public services has come under fire in the wake of recent failures such as Bechtel's at Cochabamba, Bolivia.[18] There continue to exist, amongst some, reservations regarding the wisdom of allowing private for-profit motivations to influence the provision to the public of vital resources like water.[19]

In brief, potential disadvantages of PPPs[20] include: higher project costs due to higher private sector borrowing costs or higher prescribed government payments to the private sector; transparency, accounting and evaluation issues associated with private funding; complex and costly transactions and contracts; and issues regarding competitiveness and monopolies. As will be explained in the context of the NT2 project in this monograph, it is important that both the private and public partners possess PPP-specific capacity. This requires time and experience to establish and, therefore, may create a delay to scaling up PPP procurement.[21]

B International Watercourses Law and PPPs

This section provides an outline of relevant international watercourses law at play in the context of NT2 (see Part D below for more information on NT2), and begins by explaining public international law's application to the relevant actors involved in PPPs. It summarizes applicable international treaties including the UN Convention on the Law of the Non-navigational Uses of International

---

17 See Joseph Stiglitz, 'The Post Washington Consensus,' *The Initiative for Policy Dialogue* (2004), http://intldept.uoregon.edu/wp-content/uploads/2015/03/Yarris-Joya-5.1.15-Brown-Bag-Article.pdf, accessed June 24, 2016.

18 Andrew Nickson & Claudia Vargas, 'The Limitations of Water Regulation: The Failure of the Cochabamba Concession in Bolivia,' *Bulletin of Latin American Research*, Vol. 21(1), pp. 99–120 (2002).

19 Rodrigo Cortes Rondon, 'The Law of Transnational Water Resources Projects: Transnationalism in the Brazilian Water Sector?,' (JSD Dissertation submitted to the McGeorge School of Law of the University of the Pacific, 2012). See also Pierre Guislain, 'The Privitization Challenge—A Strategic, Legal, and Institutional Analysis of International Experience,' *World Bank* (1997).

20 For a more in depth discussion on the potential benefits and disadvantages of PPPs see: Samuel Colverson & Oshani Perera, 'Harnessing the Power of Public-Private Partnerships: The Role of Hybrid Financing Strategies in Sustainable Development,' *International Institute for Sustainable Development* (2012), p. 6, http://www.iisd.org/pdf/2012/harnessing_ppp.pdf, accessed June 24, 2016; and Colverson & Perera, supra note 8, p. 4.

21 Colverson & Perera, supra note 8, p. 4.

Watercourses, and then reviews other relevant sources of the law of international watercourses that have developed over time.

I   *PPPs on International Watercourses and the Law of International Watercourses*

The law of international watercourses does not explicitly govern the actions of a private partner that would be involved in a PPP. Instead, this partner would be subject to the laws of the country in which a project is being built, while that country would be responsible to other respective riparian counterpart states under the law of international watercourses.

The public state actor would be responsible to other riparian states under international law, while the private partner would be subject to the domestic law of the host state.

(a)   State Actors

Public international law, in its traditional form, concerns itself primarily with Westphalian state actors. The traditional instruments and principles of both the UN Convention on the Law of the Non-navigational Uses of International Watercourses (the Convention) and customary international law,[22] discussed below, are concerned with states and other actors with international personality.[23] Even multinational corporations partially owned by states cannot be recognized as possessing sufficient international personality to be considered actors in the sphere of public international law.[24] Despite this lack of international legal personality, private entities can have a very real role to play

---

22   Article 32 of the Convention extends recourse to national courts to the private sphere, regardless of nationality, to address transboundary harm on an international watercourse, where harm is experienced by private individuals, either natural or juridical, in another riparian State. UN Convention on the Law of the Non-Navigational Uses of International Watercourses, UN Doc. A/RES/51/869, 21 May 1997, 36 *ILM* 700 (1997), https://treaties.un.org/doc/Publication/CN/2014/CN.271.2014-Eng.pdf, accessed June 15, 2016 [UN Watercourses Convention].

23   Some international organizations, such as the World Bank, have international personality in so far as it is bestowed by their constituent instruments.

24   In *Anglo-Iranian Oil Co* the United Kingdom argued that a concessionary contract between the Government of Iran and the Anglo-Persian Oil Company was both a contract and a treaty. The Court found that it was simply a contract between a government and a foreign corporation. A contract between a government and a multinational corporation, even as in the above case a corporation owned partially by a foreign government, cannot be considered a treaty. *Anglo-Iranian Oil Co.* (United Kingdom v. Iran), Judgment of 22 July 1952 (Preliminary Objection) [1952] ICJ Rep 2.

in transboundary waters and infrastructure development. These large infrastructure projects can have substantial transboundary effects in and on other riparian states.

The private entities involved in PPPs would fall under the domestic law of the host country. The host country, often the public element in the PPP, would be responsible for any transboundary effects originating in their country and impacting other riparian states. The arbitral tribunal in the *Trail Smelter* case found that 'no State has the right to use or permit the use of its territory in such a manner as to cause injury by fumes in or to the territory of another or the property of persons therein.'[25] Although this case dealt with air pollution, it has been found to apply to transboundary environmental effects in general and can be applied to transboundary effects on international watercourses. The *Corfu Channel* case established that it is 'every State's obligation not to allow knowingly its territory to be used for acts contrary to the rights of other States.'[26] Similarly, the *Gabčíkovo-Nagymaros Project* case found that States had a 'general obligation ... to ensure that activities within their jurisdiction and control respect the environment of other States or of areas beyond national control.'[27] This concept has been recognized as part of customary international law.[28]

II   *International Treaties*

The use and management of transboundary waters are often governed by international agreements. These agreements take precedence, to the extent they are inconsistent with otherwise applicable international norms, when interpreting legal rights regarding the use of such watercourses under the principle of *lex specialis derogate legi generali*.[29] Usually these agreements will be interpreted and function in conjunction with international customary law. The 1995 Mekong River Agreement is an example of such an agreement. This

---

25   *Trail Smelter Arbitration* (United States v. Canada), 3 R.I.A.A. 1911, 1965 (1941).
26   *Corfu Channel* (United Kingdom v. Albania), [1949] ICJ Rep 4, p. 22.
27   *Case concerning the Gabčíkovo-Nagymaros Project* (Hungary v. Slovakia), Judgment of 25 September 1997, 1997 ICJ Rep 7, para. 53, p. 41; reprinted in 37 *ILM* 162 (1998) [*Case concerning the Gabčíkovo-Nagymaros Project*].
28   Stephen McCaffrey, *The Law of International Watercourses*, Second Edition (Oxford University Press, 2007), p. 214.
29   The principle that the more specific norm governs over the more general, where the two concern the same subject matter, is often cited as an example of a general principle of international law. The Court found that the 1977 treaty governed the relationship between the parties, under *lex specialis*, in the *Case concerning the Gabčíkovo-Nagymaros Project*, supra note 27, para. 133, p. 76.

agreement, and its relationship to PPPs such as the NT2, will be explored in greater depth in Part D below.

(a)   The UN Convention on the Law of the Non-navigational Uses of International Watercourses

The UN Convention on the Law of the Non-navigational Uses of International Watercourses, adopted May 21, 1997,[30] is recognized as the most authoritative instrument in the field and a significant milestone in the development of the law of international watercourses. The Convention is largely a product of work undertaken by the International Law Commission (ILC) at the request of the UN General Assembly. The Convention finally entered into force on August 17, 2014,[31] and has thus far been ratified by 36 parties.

The Convention contains substantive and procedural obligations, with key provisions including, among others, dispute avoidance and settlement, notification of planned works, and data and information exchange. The Convention covers both the use of surface and related groundwater. Many countries would fall outside the specific force of the Convention, having not yet ratified it. However, the Convention, as a codification of the principles of international watercourses law, would be binding on states that have not yet ratified it as a principle of customary international law. Private entities are not considered under the purview of the Convention. Of particular importance are principles relating to equitable and reasonable utilization (Article 5),[32] the obligation to prevent harm[33] to other riparian states (Article 7), and planned measures on an international watercourse, set out in Part III of the Convention, specifically Article 12, the duty to notify other riparian states of planned measures with possible adverse effects.[34]

---

[30]   United Nations, 'Depositary Notification,' C.N.271.2014.TREATIES-XXVII.12, https://treaties.un.org/doc/Publication/CN/2014/CN.271.2014-Eng.pdf, accessed June 15, 2016.

[31]   UN Watercourses Convention, supra note 22.

[32]   To be considered equitable and reasonable under Article 5, a use must be consistent with adequate protection of the watercourse from pollution and other forms of degradation. Stephen McCaffrey, 'The Contribution of the UN Convention on the Law of the Non-Navigational Uses of International Watercourses,' *International Journal of Global Environmental Issues*, Vol. 1(3), pp. 250–263 (2001), p. 253.

[33]   This has been qualified as an obligation to prevent 'significant harm' by the Convention. UN Watercourses Convention, supra note 22.

[34]   "Essentially it provides that a state contemplating a new use or a change in an existing use of an international watercourse that may have a significant adverse effect on other riparian states must provide prior notification to the potentially affected states. A final important point concerning Part III is that it seems clear that, by necessity, it is premised

The term 'international watercourses' was used throughout the ILC-led process by successive rapporteurs before being incorporated into the Convention,[35] and is the original language from the UN General Assembly resolution requesting that the ILC commence work on the topic.[36] Article 2 of the Convention defines the term 'watercourse' as 'a system of surface waters and groundwaters constituting by virtue of their physical relationship a unitary whole and normally flowing into a common terminus.'[37] This term has gained wide international acceptance and incorporates connected groundwater.

The 'environmental' provisions of the Convention are contained in Part IV, 'Protection, Preservation and Management.' Article 20, 'Protection and Preservation of Ecosystems,' creates a due diligence obligation to protect and preserve watercourse ecosystems.[38] Pollution of international watercourses, marine pollution from land-based sources, and the introduction of new or alien species are dealt with in Articles 21–23 of the Convention.[39]

Articles 3 and 4 of the Convention address the Convention's relationship to other international agreements governing international watercourses. The Convention possesses a 'framework' characteristic.[40] States sharing watercourses are encouraged to adopt and adjust the Convention's provisions into specific agreements between them. The Convention does not affect existing agreements; parties to the Convention are encouraged to harmonize pre-existing agreements with the principles of the Convention, and principles embodied in the Convention will be significant in interpreting specific agreements.

Where an agreement does not include all states on a shared watercourse, the state(s) not included in the agreement's use(s) cannot be adversely affected by the agreement under Article 3 of the Convention. Where a riparian state feels the principles of the Convention should govern the use of a shared

---

on the assumption that the planning state will conduct an environmental impact assessment to identify possible adverse effects on co-riparian states". McCaffrey, supra note 32, p. 256.

35 Salman Salman, 'The World Bank Policy for Projects on International Waterways: An Historical and Legal Analysis,' Law, Justice, and Development Series No. 48741,' *World Bank Group* (2009), http://documents.worldbank.org/curated/en/276451468325130824/pdf/487410PUB0inte101OfficialoUseoOnly1.pdf, accessed June 15, 2016.
36 UN G.A. Res 2669 (XXV), UN Doc. A/8202 (December 8, 1970).
37 UN Watercourses Convention, supra note 22, art. 2.
38 McCaffrey, supra note 32, p. 256.
39 Ibid., p. 257.
40 The Convention is intended to be supplemented by more detailed agreements concerning specific watercourses. Ibid., p. 257. See also, UN Watercourses Convention, supra note 22, preamble.

watercourse, the states must enter into consultations[41] under Article 3 of the Convention.

Article 4 differentiates between international agreements that pertain to an entire international watercourse and those that apply to only a portion of a particular watercourse, or a specific project. Article 4 entitles riparian states on an international watercourse to participate in the negotiations and to become party to an agreement that applies to the entire watercourse, and to participate in consultations relating to the agreement or, where appropriate, the negotiation[42] where the riparian states' use of the watercourse may be affected by an agreement pertaining to part of the watercourse or a specific project.

Viet Nam is the only Mekong Basin state party to the Convention, having ratified it on May 19, 2014. In the process, it became the 35th party to the Convention, triggering its entry into force. All of the Lower Mekong River Basin states (including Viet Nam, Thailand, Lao PDR, and Cambodia) voted in favour of the adoption of the Convention in 1997. China, a powerful presence in regard to international watercourses and the Mekong in particular, notably was one of the three states that voted against the adoption of the Convention,[43] but it is not currently a party to the 1995 Mekong River Agreement (instead, it remains an official 'Dialogue Partner' along with Myanmar).[44]

III   *Customary International Law*

Although Viet Nam is the only Mekong Basin state that is a party to the Convention, all of the riparians would arguably still be bound by many of the tenets of the Convention in so far as they reflect customary international law. Customary international law binds international actors generally and is established through widespread and consistent practice amongst states, out of a sense of legal obligation, or *opinio juris*.

There is 'general agreement among experts in th[e] field that the provisions of the Convention reflect the basic principles of customary international water law,'[45] a sentiment shared by the International Court of Justice

---

41   '[W]ith a view to negotiating in good faith for the purpose of concluding a watercourse agreement.' UN Watercourses Convention, supra note 22, art. 3.

42   '[A]nd, where appropriate, in the negotiation thereof in good faith with a view to becoming a party thereto, to the extent that its use is thereby affected.' Ibid., art. 4.

43   United Nations General Assembly, 51st Session, 99th Plenary Meeting, UN Doc. A/51/PV.99 (May 21, 1997), p. 8; see also McCaffrey, supra note 28, p. 374.

44   McCaffrey, supra note 28, p. 286; see also pp. 286–287.

45   Salman, supra note 35, p. 57.

in the *Gabčíkovo-Nagymaros Project* case.[46] Thus many of the key provisions of the Convention largely embody the codification of existing international customary law.[47]

Besides the admittedly limited international arbitral and judicial decisions pertaining to the law of international watercourses and the Convention, much of the development of the law of international watercourses is owed to the work of two international non-governmental organizations: the Institute of International Law (IIL) and the International Law Association (ILA). Article 5 of the Convention, which deals with equitable and reasonable utilization, can be seen to build off the same concept dealt with extensively by the ILA in the Helsinki Rules.[48] By contrast the IIL developed, as a main feature of its rules and resolutions, the obligation to not cause harm to other riparians,[49] a feature that has been embodied largely in Article 7 of the Convention.

The third basic rule reflected in the Convention is that of prior notification of planned activities that may cause adverse effects in other riparian states. The Convention qualifies this as an obligation to prevent 'significant harm.'[50] These notification requirements help to prevent harm and disputes from developing down the road. These can also be viewed as a part of the equitable utilization process.[51]

IV   *Application to the Nam Theun 2 Project*

Although the framework of international law that applies to the non-navigational uses of international watercourses will be relevant for PPP projects such as NT2, its application as an area of public international law will generally apply only to the state actors involved in the project, here predominantly Lao PDR and the other downstream riparian states. The private partner of a PPP such as NT2 would fall outside of the scope of most of the tenets described above, although the concepts embodied in this area of public international law may find expression in other areas, such as the 'safeguard policies' of MDBs, which will be described in greater detail below.

While this discussion has not been an exhaustive account of the sources and structure of the law of international watercourses, it provides the reader

---

46   McCaffrey, supra note 32, pp. 259–260. See also *Case concerning the Gabčíkovo-Nagymaros Project*, supra note 27, para. 133, p. 76, and para. 85, p. 56.
47   McCaffrey, supra note 28, p. 376.
48   Salman, supra note 35, p. 54.
49   Ibid., p. 51.
50   UN Watercourses Convention, supra note 22.
51   McCaffrey, supra note 28, pp. 403–405.

with an understanding of the basic principles, sources, and structure of this area of law, which forms a vital component of the context in which major PPP infrastructure projects such as NT2 are being built.

C The Governance of PPPs through 'Policies' of Multilateral Development Banks

This section further examines the governance of PPPs by reviewing the policies of MDBs, such as the World Bank's 'safeguard policies,' which create minimum standards for Bank financed projects. 'Safeguard policies' create obligations for the Bank with respect to the management of potential impacts of infrastructure development along transboundary waterways. Thus, compliance with the safeguard policies is the responsibility of the Bank. This section traces the emerging policies of other MDBs, as well as prominent state financers of infrastructure projects such as China and the new Asia Infrastructure Investment Bank.

I *Streams of International Governance of PPPs through the World Bank Group*

In the late 1940s and early 1950s, the World Bank began devoting attention to and financing infrastructure projects on international watercourses. Due to the dearth of existing international legal norms and rules regarding international watercourses, the Bank was driven to create its own policies to follow in its decisions of whether or not to finance infrastructure projects on international watercourses. These policies, as they have evolved, have both drawn from[52] and contributed to developing the field of the international law of watercourses.[53] These policies arose partly as a function of the implicit complications and opportunities for conflict regarding projects on international watercourses, as well as due to specific objections and protests to some of the Bank's projects.[54]

---

52 Salman, supra note 35, p. 58.
53 Ibid., p. 21.
54 '[T]he first Operational Memorandum for projects on Inland International Waterways (OM 8 of 1956) was issued as a result of the objection of Turkey to the Ghab Project in Syria. The 1985 OMS was issued as result of the objection of Iran to the Igdir-Aksu Project in Turkey and the specific request of Iran that revised guidelines for projects on international waterways be issued. Moreover, as discussed earlier, the few objections that the Bank received regarding some of its financed projects were largely in the Middle East region.' Ibid., p. 50.

(a)   The World Bank's 'Safeguard' Polices

It has been argued that the World Bank's 'safeguard policies' stand out as a document relating to international watercourses for being both "a fairly comprehensive one and one with a global reach and practical application. Although it is based on the existing principles of customary international water law, the policy has made major contributions to the evolution and progressive development of such principles, and will continue to do so."[55]

In its determination of whether to finance projects on international watercourses, the Bank emphasizes its desire that riparian States reach agreement in regard to the potential project. The Bank seeks to act as a facilitator in this regard. The Bank's role on the Nile River Basin and in brokering negotiations between India and Pakistan in regard to the Indus River Basin serve as prominent examples.[56] In the event that an agreement cannot be reached, the Bank requires that the prospective borrower notify the other riparians of the project, while specifying detailed procedures that such notification must follow.[57]

As noted in Part B above, the ILC used, and subsequently enshrined in the Convention, the term 'watercourse.' The ILA instead used the term 'drainage basin.' The Bank, early in its deliberations around policy on international watercourses, had to grapple with defining the terms it would use and the corresponding scope of the policy. In Operational Memorandum ('OM') 8, the Bank used the term 'waterways' but moved away from this term in 1965, only to return to 'waterways' later on.[58] The use of the term 'waterways' by the Bank persists to this day and is used to refer to semi-enclosed coastal waters, closed seas, and national rivers flowing into those waters, and is absent explicit provisions on transboundary groundwater.[59] 'Waterways' was traditionally a term associated with navigation,[60] while the other terms have been associated more with non-navigational uses.

The use of the term waterways shows a departure from the wider stream of international legal nomenclature. This illustrates the unique role that the Bank plays as both an international cooperative financial institution and a pioneer

---

55   Ibid., p. 236.
56   *Indus Waters Kishenganga Arbitration* (Pakistan v. India) (Partial Award) (Permanent Court of Arbitration, February 18, 2013), pp. 44–45, https://pcacases.com/web/send Attach/1681, accessed June 15, 2016.
57   See *Operational Manual BP 7.50—Projects on International Waterways*, World Bank Group (March 2012), https://policies.worldbank.org/sites/ppf3/PPFDocuments/Forms/DispPage.aspx?docid=1843, accessed June 22, 2017.
58   Salman, supra note 35, p. 46.
59   Ibid., pp. 79, 88.
60   McCaffrey, supra note 28, p. 38.

that can influence the practical evolution of international norms.⁶¹ Although, as it stands now, the failure to include linked groundwater in 'waterways' may be unduly limiting, compared to the more widely used 'watercourses.'

The Bank drew upon its operational policies and in 1997 created ten policies termed the 'safeguard policies'. These 'policies', which have subsequently been updated, deal with⁶² environmental assessment (OP/BP 4.01); natural habitats (OP/BP 4.04); forests (OP/BP 4.36); pest management (OP 4.09); safety of dams (OP/BP 4.37); physical cultural resources (OP/BP 4.11); involuntary resettlement (OP/BP 4.12); indigenous peoples (OP/BP 4.10); projects on international waterways (OP/BP 7.50); and projects in disputed areas (OP/BP 7.60).⁶³

The presence of OP/BP 7.50 as a 'safeguard policy' pertaining to international waterways is somewhat unique among MDBs and illustrates both the importance of projects on international waterways to the World Bank and the potential risk that these projects can present on important waterways. The necessity of a policy devoted to projects on international waterways shows the special nature of these projects and their unique requirements and surrounding issues.

On August 4, 2016, the World Bank's Board of Executive Directors approved a new Environmental and Social Framework (the 'Framework') for Bank-financed investment projects.⁶⁴ The Framework replaced several of the previous Bank 'safeguard policies,'⁶⁵ but did not replace OP/BP 7.50 or OP/BP 7.60.

---

61 Salman, supra note 35, p. 88.
62 Ibid., p. 60.
63 Ibid., p. 60, note 194.
64 *Review and Update of World Bank Safeguard Policies*, World Bank Group, https://consultations.worldbank.org/consultation/review-and-update-world-bank-safeguard-policies, accessed September 23, 2016; 'World Bank Board Approves New Environmental and Social Framework,' *World Bank Group* (August 4, 2016), http://www.worldbank.org/en/news/press-release/2016/08/04/world-bank-board-approves-new-environmental-and-social-framework, accessed September 24, 2016.
65 'This Framework replaces the following Operational Policy (OP) and Bank Procedures (BP): OP/BP4.00, Piloting the Use of Borrower Systems to Address Environmental and Social Safeguard Issues in Bank-Supported Projects, OP/BP4.01, Environmental Assessment, OP/BP4.04, Natural Habitats, OP4.09, Pest Management, OP/BP4.10, Indigenous Peoples, OP/BP4.11, Physical Cultural Resources, OP/BP4.12, Involuntary Resettlement, OP/BP4.36, Forests, and OP/BP4.37, Safety of Dams. This Framework does not replace OP/BP4.03, Performance Standards for Private Sector Activities, OP/BP7.50, Projects on International Waterways, and OP/BP7.60, Projects in Disputed Territories.' World Bank Environmental and Social Framework: Setting Environmental and Social Standards for Investment Project Financing,' *World Bank Group* (August 4, 2016), para. 13, p. 3, https://consultations.worldbank.org/Data/hub/files/consultation-template/review-and-update-world-bank-

In announcing the updated policies, the Bank noted that 'the framework brings the World Bank's environmental and social protections into closer harmony with those of other development institutions, and makes important advances in areas such as transparency, non-discrimination, social inclusion, public participation, and accountability—including expanded roles for grievance redress mechanisms.'[66] The Framework sets out mandatory requirements that apply to the Bank in the World Bank Environmental and Social Policy for Investment Project Financing.[67] The Framework adopts ten Environmental and Social Safeguards, which set out mandatory requirements for borrowers and projects in the following areas:

1. Assessment and management of environmental and social risks and impacts
2. Labor and working conditions
3. Resource efficiency and pollution prevention and management
4. Community health and safety
5. Land acquisition, restrictions on land use and involuntary resettlement
6. Biodiversity conservation and sustainable management of living natural resources
7. Indigenous peoples/Sub-Saharan African historically underserved traditional local communities
8. Cultural heritage
9. Financial intermediaries
10. Stakeholder engagement and information disclosure[68]

(b) Other Safeguard Policies

As listed above there are now several 'safeguard policies' in existence, outside those outlined in OP/BP 7.50. Several of these policies could be applicable in the context of a large-scale infrastructure project on an international watercourse, such as NT2. However, due to the focus on the law of international watercourses and the constraints of this monograph, these other policies have

---

safeguard-policies/en/materials/the_esf_clean_final_for_public_disclosure_post_board_august_4.pdf, accessed September 24, 2016.
66 'World Bank Board Approves New Environmental and Social Framework,' supra note 64.
67 World Bank, supra note 65, para. 2, p. 1.
68 Ibid., p. 1.

been noted here but will not be a discussed further. The large scale of NT2 meant that all ten of the 'safeguard policies' of the World Bank were triggered.[69]

(c)   Substantive Obligations
(i)   *Notification*

One of the central elements of the World Bank's 'safeguard policies' with respect to international waters is the requirement to notify riparian States of the proposed project on a shared waterway. The policies set out clear procedures that must be followed. This requirement is triggered if a project meets the specific requirements of scope and is planned on a specific type of shared waterway, or will affect a shared waterway, subject to three limited exceptions.[70] Once the notification requirement is triggered there is no *de minimus* standard in regard to the project's expected impacts, and notification must be given.[71] The obligation to notify falls to the proponent of a specific project; if the proponent is unable or unwilling to provide notice, the Bank will act in its capacity as a liaison and provide notice to riparian states. If the proponent is unwilling to allow this form of notice, the project is either redesigned, so it no longer requires notification, or Bank financing is withdrawn.[72]

The requirement to notify other riparians of proposed measures is a concept that has been incorporated into the law of international watercourses both through customary international law[73] and instruments like the Convention. The arbitral tribunal in the *Lake Lanoux* decision found: 'A state wishing to do that which will affect an international watercourse cannot decide whether another state's interest will be affected; the other state is the sole judge of that and has the right to information on the proposals.'[74] Through its notice requirements, the Bank allows potentially affected riparians to inform the Bank of their own assessment of harm in regard to a proposed project.

---

69   Ian C. Porter & Jayasankar Shivakumar (eds), *Doing a Dam Better: The Lao People's Democratic Republic and the Story of Nam Theun 2* (World Bank, 2011), p. 18, http://documents.worldbank.org/curated/en/200041468044952974/pdf/584400PUB0ID161Bettero9780821369852.pdf, accessed June 22, 2016.

70   These exceptions include rehabilitations of existing schemes, water resources surveys and feasibility studies, and projects in a tributary exclusively in the lowest downstream riparian. See Salman, supra note 35, pp. 162–180.

71   Ibid., p. 109.

72   Ibid., p. 235.

73   '[T]he Bank seems to follow closely the *ratio decidendi* of the *Lake Lanoux* arbitral award, which stated that it is the other riparian, and not the state planning an activity, that should decide whether its interests are affected, and should thus be provided with information on the proposed project to enable it to make that decision.' Ibid., p. 233.

74   *Lake Lanoux Arbitration* (France v. Spain), 24 *ILR* 101 (1957) at 130.

The Bank's requirements for notification are expressly extended to non-members of the World Bank.

> It is necessary because of the general obligation under international law to avoid harm to all other riparians. This is a basic obligation that the Bank could not possibly overlook. By making an explicit reference to non-members, the Bank is simply emphasizing and underscoring this obligation.[75]

Also of particular importance, for our purposes, is the Bank's lack of distinction between upstream or downstream riparians in regard to the notice requirements. The 'safeguard policies' require notice to *all* riparians. This recognizes the concept that impacts and harm can flow both upstream and downstream.[76] In particular, upstream impacts can be the foreclosure of future uses of water by the upstream state if the downstream state applies all the flow requirements of watercourse to their own uses. Arguably these downstream uses would then be significantly harmed by any upstream uses that would take away from the water required by the downstream state for its uses. This idea is also embodied in the Convention and, arguably, is also integrated into customary international law, which requires notice of proposed measures on international watercourses regardless of whether riparian states are upstream or downstream. The Bank's notice requirements in practical application can be seen to form a confluence between the concepts of the obligation to not cause appreciable harm and the principle of equitable and reasonable utilization.[77]

> It is true that the ILA Helsinki Rules and the UN Watercourses Convention both require notification to other watercourse states, without limiting the requirement to downstream riparians. However, the Bank policy has clarified this matter through the practical application of the requirement of notification of all the riparians and through providing such riparians with the opportunity to determine the effects of the project on their interests on the shared waterway. This is, no doubt, a significant and major contribution of the policy to the evolution and progressive development of international water law.[78]

---

75 Salman, supra note 35, p. 33.
76 Ibid., p. 229.
77 Ibid., pp. 104, 229.
78 Ibid., p. 230.

(ii)   *No Harm*

As mentioned above, the Bank's policy is based on the obligation not to cause 'appreciable harm' to other riparians.[79] Though there is a difference in the language used, 'significant harm' is used in the Convention, both phrases can be seen to embody the same normative principle. In discussions of the IIL surrounding the creation of the language that would become the Convention, 'appreciable harm' was used, though ultimately, the IIL decided to utilize 'significant harm.'[80] The concept of 'no harm' favoured by the IIL has now been codified into the Convention and arguably adopted as norm of customary international law. Overall, the Bank's policies can be seen to be in keeping with this general stream of international norms in the area of international watercourses.

II   *Other Multilateral Development Banks*

There are several other MDBs that have their own equivalents to the World Bank's 'safeguard policies'; however, the World Bank is the only international financial institution that has a specific and detailed policy dealing with projects on international waterways.[81] Due to the constraints of space, the discussion in this monograph focuses solely on the 'safeguard policies' of the World Bank.

Several other MDBs were involved in NT2, and their involvement will be discussed in greater depth below. As will be discussed, the equivalent 'safeguard policies' of the other MDBs involved in the project were applied in conjunction with those of the World Bank. These 'parallel policies' could complicate compliance by proponent states and private parties, though attempts to streamline the due diligence work did occur in this specific case.[82] Some examples of other multilateral development banks are the Asian Development Bank (ADB),[83] the

---

79   Ibid., p. 104.
80   Salman Salman, & Laurence Boisson de Chazournes, 'International Water Courses, Enhancing Cooperation and Managing Conflict, Proceedings of a World Bank Seminar,' World Bank Technical Paper No. 414, *World Bank Group* (1998), http://documents.worldbank.org/curated/en/496071468223476867/pdf/WTP14multiopage.pdf.
81   Salman, supra note 35, p. 64.
82   Porter & Shivakumar, supra note 69, p. 83.
83   See *Operations Manual*, Asian Development Bank (ADB), http://www.adb.org/documents/operations-manual, accessed June 22, 2016. Contained in these operational policies are three areas of safeguard policies: (i) environmental safeguards, (ii) involuntary resettlement safeguards, and (iii) indigenous peoples safeguards. The ADB categorizes projects based on likely level of impacts. See also 'Operations Manual: Bank Policies,' *Asian Development Bank* (2013), http://www.adb.org/sites/default/files/institutional-document/31483/om-f1–20131001.pdf, accessed June 22, 2016.

Asian Infrastructure Investment Bank (AIIB),[84] the European Investment Bank (EIB),[85] and the Nordic Investment Bank (NIB).[86] The ADB, EIB, and NIB were all involved in the financing of NT2.

III   The International Finance Corporation's Performance Standards

The IFC is not bound by the 'safeguard policies' discussed above, as they only apply to the International Bank for Reconstruction and Development and the International Development Association (IDA). The IFC, which lends directly to, and makes equity investments in, private companies and projects in member countries,[87] has its own distinct equivalent of the Bank's 'safeguard policies.'[88]

The current IFC social policies, called 'Performance Standards' (PS), were adopted in 2012. These standards, to a large extent, have covered similar issues to those addressed in the Bank's 'safeguard policies'.[89] In total eight PS and

---

84   See below for discussion on the AIIB.

85   The European Investment Bank (EIB) requires compliance with national legislation and regulations as well as obligations under relevant international agreements and specific UN international agreements. The EIB may also require various environmental and social assessments. The EIB differentiates between European Union (EU), EU candidate and potential candidate countries, and non-EU countries. The EIB articulates environmental and social standards divided across ten thematic areas. See, 'Environmental and Social Practices Handbook,' Version 9.0, *European Investment Bank, Environment, Climate & Social Office Projects Directorate* (2013), http://www.eib.org/attachments/strategies/environmental_and_social_practices_handbook_en.pdf, accessed June 22, 2016.

86   The Nordic Investment Bank (NIB) assesses the social and environmental impacts of all loan applications in light of the NIB's 'Sustainability Policy and Guidelines' and may reject applications for non-compliance. The NIB also uses the IFC and World Bank Group's policies and guidelines as benchmarks. The NIB requires compliance with various EU legislation and is a signatory of the European Principles on the Environment. The NIB draws a distinction between projects inside the European Union or the European Economic Area and those outside. The NIB also requires compliance with national laws in a host state as well as compliance with relevant international agreements. See 'Sustainability Policy and Guidelines,' *Nordic Investment Bank* (2012), pp. 3, 5, 7–8, http://www.nib.int/filebank/56-Sustainability_Policy_Guidelines-2012.pdf, accessed June 22, 2016.

87   *Our Funding: We raise capital through bond issuances*, International Finance Corporation, World Bank Group, http://www.ifc.org/wps/wcm/connect/corp_ext_content/ifc_external_corporate_site/about+ifc_new/ifc+governance/funding/ourfunding, accessed June 22, 2016.

88   See *Environmental and Social Performance Standards and Guidance Notes*, International Finance Corporation, World Bank Group, http://www.ifc.org/wps/wcm/connect/topics_ext_content/ifc_external_corporate_site/ifc+sustainability/our+approach/risk+management/performance+standards/environmental+and+social+performance+standards+and+guidance+notes, accessed June 22, 2016.

89   Salman, supra note 35, p. 62.

accompanying 'Guidance Notes' (GN), which provide implementation guidance to IFC clients, have been adopted by the IFC. IFC Operational Policy 7.50 governed projects on international waterways and drew heavily from the Bank's 'safeguard policy.'[90] However, in 2006, Operational Policy 7.50 was replaced by the IFC's policy on social and environmental sustainability.[91] The 2012 policy articulates the identification of risks and impacts required by the client[92] including "potential transboundary effects, such as pollution of air, or use or pollution of international waterways".[93]

The World Bank stands out for its detailed policies and procedures for projects on international waterways. Although the IFC and the Multilateral Investment Guarantee Agency (MIGA) now have their own policies, it is likely that the general provisions included therein will be complemented by the detailed provisions as well as the precedents and practice of the World Bank.[94]

The 'equator principles' are a private finance industry standard based upon the IFC PS. A growing number of institutions are adopting[95] these 'principles' as a financial industry benchmark for determining, assessing, and managing risk, both social and environmental, in international project development and finance.[96] Their adoption represents the proliferation of governance norms to private industry and project finance globally, entrenching these norms in the vocabulary of industry and global finance generally.

The eight IFC Performance Standards have been adopted by the World Bank as the *Performance Standards for Projects Supported by the Private Sector* (OP/

---

90 Ibid.

91 Ibid.

92 "The term "client" is used throughout the Performance Standards broadly to refer to the party responsible for implementing and operating the project that is being financed, or the recipient of the financing, depending on the project structure and type of financing." 'Performance Standards on Environmental and Social Sustainability,' *International Finance Corporation, World Bank Group*, (2012), p. i, footnote 1, http://www.ifc.org/wps/wcm/connect/115482804a0255db96fbffd1a5d13d27/PS_English_2012_Full-Document.pdf?MOD=AJPERES, accessed July 21, 2017.

93 Ibid., p. 3, para 7, http://www.ifc.org/wps/wcm/connect/115482804a0255db96fbffd1a5d13d27/PS_English_2012_Full-Document.pdf?MOD=AJPERES, accessed July 21, 2017.

94 Salman, supra note 35, p. 64.

95 As of December 16, 2016, 87 institutions have adopted the 'equator principles.' See Christopher Wright & Alexis Rwabizambuga, 'Institutional pressures, corporate reputation, and voluntary codes of conduct: An examination of the equator principles,' *Business and Society Review*, Vol. 111(1), pp. 89–117, (2006).

96 Salman, supra note 35, p. 63.

BP 4.03).[97] The World Bank PS apply to Bank support for projects (or components thereof) that are designed, owned, constructed, and/or operated by a private entity in lieu of the Bank's 'safeguard policies.' These standards are seen to be 'better suited to the private sector, while enhancing greater policy coherence and cooperation across the World Bank Group.'[98] It seems that this could be viewed as an erosion of normative governance for PPP projects on international watercourses as the World Bank PS and IFC PS lack a specific policy covering projects on international waterways, as is contained in the Bank's 'safeguard policies'. Further, there could be a situation when both IFC (or MIGA) 'Performance Standards' and World Bank safeguard policies apply to a given project.[99]

IV   China and Chinese Development

The World Bank is now facing greater competition internationally, especially from the growing power and presence of China as a financier of infrastructure globally. The Bank has seen its pre-eminence in international dam project finance slip in recent years; it is reported that although the Bank has increased its financing to about '[US]$1.8 billion in 2014, it still funds only 2 percent of hydropower project investment today.'[100] China has emerged as a global leader in financing dams, which is driven by a variety of economic engines. The China Export-Import Bank (China Exim Bank), founded in 1994, has emerged as one of the world's largest export credit agencies. The Chinese Development Bank (CDB), wholly owned by the Chinese government,[101] has a large presence in current 'international infrastructure project finance. Further, Sinohydro 'is leading the global hydropower sector as the world's largest dam company in

---

97   *Operational Manual OP 4.03, Performance Standards for Private Sector Activities*, World Bank Group (2013), https://policies.worldbank.org/sites/ppf3/PPFDocuments/090224 b0822f7442.pdf, accessed June 15, 2016.
98   Ibid., p. 1.
99   See 'World Bank Performance Standards for Private Sector Activities, Guidance Note,' *World Bank Group*, http://siteresources.worldbank.org/EXTSAFEPOL/Resources/OPBP 4.03GNApr22Webclean.pdf?resourceurlname=OPBP4.03GNApr22Webclean.pdf, accessed September 24, 2016.
100 Erica Gies, 'A Dam Revival, Despite Risks,' *The New York Times* (November 19, 2014), http://www.nytimes.com/2014/11/20/business/energy-environment/private-funding-brings-a-boom-in-hydropower-with-high-costs.html?_r=1, accessed September 24, 2016.
101 Henry Sanderson & Michael Forsythe, *China's Superbank. Debt, Oil and Influence—How China Development Bank is Rewriting the Rules of Finance* (Wiley-Bloomberg Press, 2013), p. 163.

terms of number and size of dams built, investment sums and global coverage.'[102] Some sources claim that China is now the predominant financier and builder of dams worldwide.[103]

In contrast to private equity in the western world, China's state backing can be seen to represent a blending of lines between the private and public spheres. China represents the second largest private equity market in the world after the United States, with approximately US$30 billion in investments.[104] The effect of this market on international investment and the governance of PPPs on international watercourses will be profound. It is also worth questioning if a blending of public and private funds in the form of Chinese investment and projects creates a greater need to assess what tools govern PPPs and to extend international legal norms to these partnerships, as state actors may use private corporations, wholly owned by them, to separate themselves directly from international legal norms.

(a)   The Asian Infrastructure Investment Bank

Another element in China's global infrastructure activities has been the relatively recent creation of the Asian Infrastructure Investment Bank. The AIIB is a MDB that allocates the largest interest to China but has many shareholder states, including traditional American allies such as Britain and Singapore.[105] To a certain extent, the AIIB normalizes Chinese investment in the developing world and provides an opportunity for these investments to go through less opaque channels, subjecting them to scrutiny from the AIIB's other members.[106] There is anxiety over the growing power and assertiveness of Chinese investment

---

102   Frauke Urban et al., 'South-South Technology Transfer of Low-Carbon Innovation: Large Chinese Hydropower Dams in Cambodia,' *Sustainable Development*, Vol. 23(4), pp. 232–244, (2015), p. 234, http://onlinelibrary.wiley.com/doi/10.1002/sd.1590/full, accessed June 15, 2016.

103   International Rivers, 'The New Great Walls: a Guide to China's Oversea Dam Industry,' Second Edition, *International Rivers* (2012), pp. 1–2, https://www.internationalrivers.org/sites/default/files/attached-files/intlrivers_newgreatwalls_2012_2.pdf, accessed June 15, 2016.

104   Sanderson & Forsythe, supra note 102, p. 163.

105   'The Asian Infrastructure Investment Bank: The Infrastructure Gap,' *The Economist* (March 21, 2015), http://www.economist.com/news/asia/21646740-development-finance-helps-china-win-friends-and-influence-american-allies-infrastructure-gap, accessed June 15, 2016.

106   Kenneth Rogoff, 'Will China's Infrastructure Bank Work?,' *The Guardian* (April 7, 2015), http://www.theguardian.com/business/2015/apr/07/will-chinas-infrastructure-bank-work, accessed June 15, 2016.

represented by the AIIB, as well as the strength of governance standards that the AIIB employs.[107] Some commentators feel the AIIB may provide an opportunity to put China into a leadership role, as well as to pull them closer to compliance with various international norms.[108]

On April 13, 2016, the World Bank and the AIIB signed their first co-financing framework agreement to jointly develop projects. When this agreement was made, the two banks were discussing nearly a dozen co-financed projects.[109]

In February 2016, the AIIB adopted its own Environmental and Social Framework,[110] setting out its governing environmental and social policy and associated mandatory environmental and social standards, including consideration of environmental and social assessment and management; involuntary resettlement; and indigenous peoples.[111] The adoption of an Environmental and Social Framework similar to that of the World Bank is promising for normative governance and financing of large infrastructure projects internationally.

D   The Mekong River Basin, the 1995 Mekong Agreement and the Nam Theun 2 Hydropower Project

This section situates NT2 within the geographical context of the Mekong River Basin. The shared use of this international watercourse is governed in part by the 1995 Mekong Agreement, which creates an institutional framework for cooperation among states. This section provides an overview of this governance structure, including how administrative costs are financed, how data and information are exchanged, and how disputes are resolved. A summary of key initiatives launched since the 1995 Mekong Agreement came into existence is

---

107   Nicholas Watt, Paul Lewis, & Tania Branigan, 'US Anger at Britain Joining Chinese Led Investment Bank AIIB,' *The Guardian* (March 13, 2015), http://www.theguardian.com/us-news/2015/mar/13/white-house-pointedly-asks-uk-to-use-its-voice-as-part-of-chinese-led-bank, accessed June 15, 2016.
108   'The Asian Infrastructure Investment Bank: The Infrastructure Gap,' supra note 104. See also Rogoff, supra note 107.
109   'World Bank and AIIB sign First Co-Financing Framework Agreement,' *World Bank Group* (April 13, 2016), http://www.worldbank.org/en/news/press-release/2016/04/13/world-bank-and-aiib-sign-first-co-financing-framework-agreement, accessed September 24, 2016.
110   'Asian Infrastructure Investment Bank Environmental and Social Framework,' *Asian Infrastructure Investment Bank* (2016), http://www.aiib.org/uploadfile/2016/0226/20160226043633542.pdf, accessed September 24, 2016.
111   Ibid., p. 1.

also provided. Finally, the development, history and implementation of NT2 is discussed. The section concludes by summarizing the impacts and significance of NT2, addressing both its effects on the Lao PDR economy and the internal capacity it developed, as well as the policies and practices of the World Bank.

I   NT2 is Located in Lao PDR in the Mekong River Basin

The Mekong River Basin spans an area 795,000 km² over six countries—China, Myanmar, Lao PDR, Thailand, Cambodia, and Viet Nam. The Mekong is the twelfth longest river in the world (4,350 km), ranking tenth in terms of total volume (475 billion m³/year), and has the second highest diversity of plant and animal life after the Amazon River.[112] The Mekong is dominated by a monsoon climate with distinct wet and dry seasons, and it serves as a vital transportation network, key source of protein in the diets of the riparian states, and holds vast hydroelectric potential. Most of the total flow volume is delivered to the Mekong from tributaries in the lower Mekong Basin with upstream China contributing over 24% of the total flow from snow melt in the dry season.[113]

The Mekong River Basin has been the subject of considerable international efforts to spur regional cooperation dating back to the original Mekong Committee that was established in the 1950s. It was then described as the "largest single development project that the fledgling United Nations organization had ever undertaken."[114] However, in the following 37 years, in spite of various institutional arrangements, intensive investigation, and planning, no structures have been built on the mainstream of the Lower Mekong River. This phenomenon can be partly explained by the geopolitical barriers and, at times, outright conflict between the riparian states.

II   1995 Agreement on the Cooperation for the Sustainable Development of the Mekong River Basin

The 1995 Mekong Agreement is a treaty among the states of Cambodia, Lao PDR, Thailand, and Viet Nam, collectively described as the 'Lower Mekong River Basin States' (LMRBS), to provide a framework for cooperation in the 'sustainable development, utilization, conservation and management of the

---

112   *Natural Resources*, Mekong River Commission, http://www.mrcmekong.org/mekong-basin/natural-resources/, accessed July 28, 2016.

113   *Hydrology*, Mekong River Commission, http://www.mrcmekong.org/mekong-basin/hydrology/, accessed July 28, 2016.

114   *History*, Mekong River Commission, http://www.mrcmekong.org/about-mrc/history/, accessed July 28, 2016.

Mekong River Basin waters and related resources.'[115] The LMRBS have signed and ratified the 1995 Mekong Agreement, which entered into force on April 5, 1995. The 1995 Mekong Agreement reflects a number of the key principles enshrined in both in the UN Watercourses Convention and customary international water law.

As one of the few legally-binding treaties in Southeast Asia, the 1995 Mekong Agreement was the outcome of concerted regional and supra-regional efforts over 37 years to develop a system to cooperatively manage the Mekong River.[116] The 1995 Mekong Agreement established the Mekong River Commission (MRC) as the regional management body for the Basin, replacing the existing Interim Mekong Committee. The MRC was given the responsibility to coordinate the development of water resources in relation to the natural resources and environmental protection in the Lower Mekong River Basin.[117]

China and Myanmar, the upstream riparians in the Mekong, are currently 'Dialogue Partners,' rather than full parties, to the 1995 Mekong Agreement. Should China and Myanmar wish to become full parties to the 1995

---

115 Agreement on the Cooperation for the Sustainable Development of the Mekong River Basin, 5 April 1995, Kingdom of Cambodia, Lao People's Democratic Republic, Kingdom of Thailand, and the Socialist Republic of Viet Nam, art. 1, http://www.mrcmekong.org/assets/Publications/policies/agreement-Apr95.pdf, accessed July 28, 2016 [1995 Mekong Agreement]. For additional background and analysis of the 1995 Mekong Agreement see, Richard Kyle Paisley, Patrick Weiler, & Taylor Henshaw, Transboundary International Waters Governance Through the Prism of the Mekong River Basin,' *in*, Janice Gray, Cameron Holley, & Rosemary Rayfuse (eds), *Trans-jurisdictional Water Law and Governance*, pp. 43–61 (Earthscan Studies in Water Resource Management Routledge, Taylor & Francis Group, 2016).

116 Joakim Öjendal & Kurt Jensen, 'Politics and Development of the Mekong River Basin: Trans-boundary Dilemmas and Participatory Ambitions,' *in*, Joakim Öjendal, Stina Hansson, & Sofie Hellberg (eds), *Politics and Development in a Trans-boundary Watershed: The Case of the Lower Mekong Basin*, pp. 37–59 (Springer, 2012).

117 Greg Browder, '*Negotiating an International Regime for Water Allocation in the Mekong River Basin*,' (Unpublished PhD dissertation, Stanford University, 1998).

Agreement—which many believe is necessary for the 1995 Mekong Agreement to fully realize its purpose and set goals[118]—they have the potential to do so.[119]

China completed its first dam on the river in the year the 1995 Mekong Agreement was signed. Since that time, China has completed another six of 37 dams it has planned for the Lancang/Upper Mekong.[120] The rapid hydroelectric development in China has had a significant effect on the Mekong River water and sedimentation levels, and therefore presents both a great opportunity and environmental risk to the Basin. For this reason, increasing engagement from China has been seen as a critical factor in the success of the 1995 Mekong Agreement.

(a)   Structure of the MRC

The 1995 Mekong Agreement creates the MRC as the 'institutional framework for cooperation in the Mekong River Basin.'[121] Figure 2 sets out the structure of the MRC.

Three main bodies make up the MRC: the Council, the Joint Committee (JC), and the Secretariat. The Council consists of a representative at the ministerial or cabinet level from each Member State, meets annually, and is responsible for overall governance of the MRC.[122]

One person from a rank that is no less than the level of head of department is appointed by each country to serve on the JC. The JC is responsible for the implementation of Council decisions and policies and, as such, functions as a sort of management board. Importantly, and as will be discussed

---

118 See Aaron Wolf & Joshua Newton, 'Case Study Transboundary Dispute Resolution: the Mekong Committee,' *Program in Water Conflict Management and Transformation* (2007), http://www.transboundarywaters.orst.edu/research/case_studies/Documents/mekong.pdf, accessed July 28, 2016; Ellen Backer, 'The Mekong River Commission: Does it work, and how does the Mekong Basin's geography influence its effectiveness?,' *Südostasien Aktuell*, Vol. 26(4), pp. 31–55, (2007).

119 1995 Mekong Agreement, supra note 116, art. 39: '[a]ny other riparian State, accepting the rights and obligations under this Agreement, may become a party with the consent of the parties.'

120 'The ISH 0306 Study: Development of Guidelines for Hydropower Environmental Impact Mitigation and Risk Management in the Lower Mekong Mainstream and Tributaries,' *Mekong River Commission* (2015), p. 16, http://www.mrcmekong.org/assets/Publications/policies/1st-Interim-Report-ISH0306-Volume-1-The-Guidelines-Final.pdf, accessed July 28, 2016.

121 1995 Mekong Agreement, supra note 116, art. 11.

122 Ibid., c. IV, arts. 11–33;*Organisational Structure*, Mekong River Commission, http://www.mrcmekong.org/about-mrc/organisational-structure/, accessed July 28, 2016.

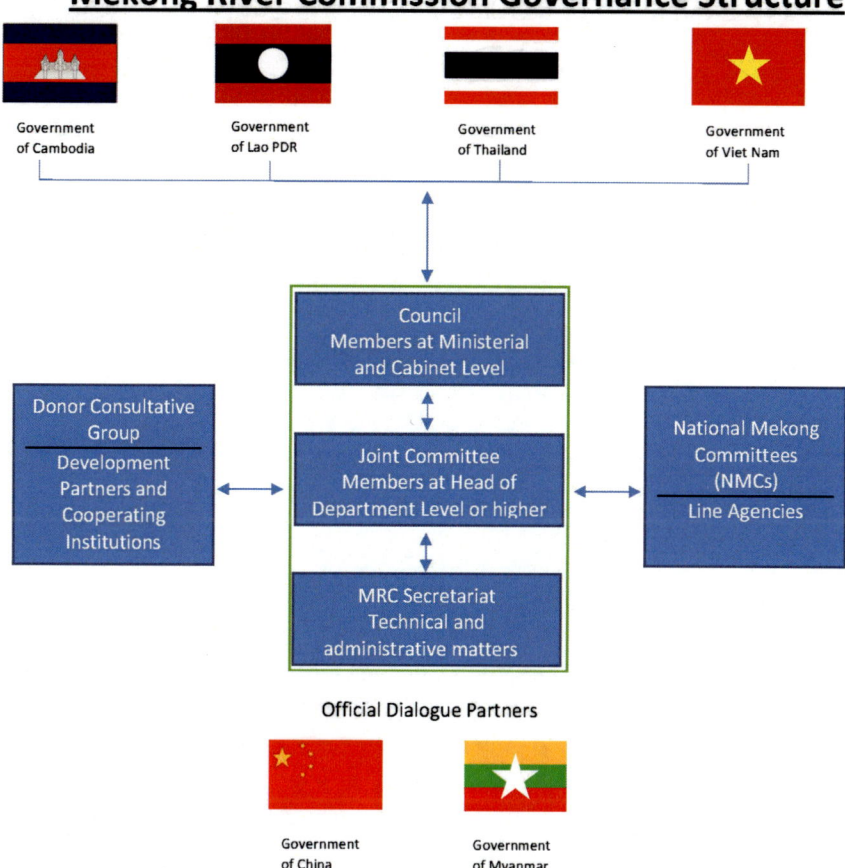

FIGURE 2   *Mekong River Commission governance structure.*

further below, the JC is responsible for the implementation of the 1995 Mekong Agreement and the Basin Development Plan (BDP), including periodic assessments of their successes.

The Secretariat is the main operational arm of the MRC, providing technical, logistical, and administrative assistance to the MRC. The Secretariat is made up of 150 staff based out of offices in Phnom Penh, Cambodia, and Vientiane, Lao PDR, and is directed by a Council-appointed Chief Executive Officer.

The MRC is supported by the National Mekong Committees, which coordinate activities at the national level for each of the parties to the 1995 Mekong Agreement and form a crucial link to national ministries and agencies. While China and Myanmar are not official parties to the MRC, China provides water

FIGURE 3   *Mekong River Commission secretariat operational structure.*

level data during flood season from stations located within its boundaries on the Upper Mekong.

In addition to Member States, the 'Dialogue Partners' and some international organizations[123] have the right to attend and participate in the one-day annual fall meeting of the JC and Council meetings. Donors have the opportunity of dialoguing and coordinating with the MRC through the Donor Consultative Group. There are currently 15 development partners[124] and eight contributing organizations. The contributing organizations work with the MRC under jointly funded projects through memorandum of understanding or in research capacities.

(b)   Financing

The MRC administrative costs are financed by equal contributions from each of its Member States (Art. 14). However, the MRC is heavily reliant on

---

123   These organizations include the Asian Development Bank, Association of Southeast Asian Nations (ASEAN), International Union for Conservation of Nature (IUCN), United Nations Development Programme (UNDP), United Nations Economic and Social Commission for Asia and the Pacific (UNESCAP), World Bank (WB), and World Wildlife Fund (WWF). See *Development Partners & Partner Organisations*, Mekong River Commission, http://www.mrcmekong.org/about-mrc/development-partners-and-partner-organisations/, accessed July 28, 2016.

124   Australia, Belgium, Denmark, European Union, Finland, France, Germany, Japan, Luxembourg, New Zealand, Sweden, Switzerland, the Netherlands, the United States, and the World Bank.

international donors to fund its projects and programmes.[125] 'Development Partners' have pledged more than US$20 million for the 2016–2020 strategic planning period for the MRC.[126]

(c)   Data and Information Exchange

In the 40 years prior to the inception of the MRC, there had been varying levels of data and information exchange among the LMRBS. As a result, the 1995 Mekong Agreement served to cement an existing process by empowering MRC bodies, rather than forging an entirely new process from scratch.[127] However, the framework only set out very general terms for data collection and information exchange.

(d)   Flexibility

The MRC seeks to balance two often contrasting objectives with respect to the use of Mekong River waters: 1) the need to maintain ecological integrity in varying environmental conditions; and, 2) the respect of territorial sovereignty. The 1995 Agreement accomplishes these two goals by instilling flexible decision-making processes while protecting the fundamental interests of the parties through its procedural requirements.[128]

A poignant example is the dynamic operational decision-making processes related to 'reasonable and equitable utilization' of the Mekong as provided by

---

125   For example, in the period 2013–2014, donors contributed US$29,069,102, whereas, the riparian governments contributed US$4,830,504. See 'Financial Statements and Independent Auditors' Report Year ended 31 December 2014,' *Mekong River Commission* (2015), p. 7, http://www.mrcmekong.org/assets/Publications/governance/Part-II-MRC-FS-Audit-2014-FINAL.pdf, accessed July 28, 2016.

126   Federico Rodriguez, 'Annual Report 2014: Mekong River Commission,' *Mekong River Commission*, (2015), p. 49, http://www.mrcmekong.org/assets/Publications/governance/MRC-Annual-Report-2014.pdf, accessed July 25, 2016. In recognition of this essential donor involvement, Article 41 of the 1995 Mekong Agreement specifically acknowledges the contributions of the United Nations and the international community, and expresses the desire to continue these relationships.

127   1995 Mekong Agreement, supra note 116, see Article 24, which provides that the JC is to 'regularly obtain, update and exchange information and data necessary to implement this Agreement' and 'conduct appropriate studies and assessments for the protection of the environment and maintenance of the ecological balance of the Mekong River Basin' and Article 30, which directs the Secretariat to '[m]aintain databases of information as directed.'

128   Susanne Schmeier, 'Resilience to Climate Change-Induced Challenges in the Mekong River Basin: The Role of the MRC,' *World Bank Group* (2011), http://documents.worldbank.org/curated/en/630751468330303325/Resilience-to-climate-change-induced-challenges-in-the-Mekong-river-basin-the-role-of-the-MRC, accessed July 24, 2016.

Article 5. Based on the season or the intended use of the Mekong and its tributaries, different procedural steps are prescribed in discussions that occur at the JC level. Importantly, Article 5 notes that any use of the tributaries or intra-basin uses of the mainstream in the wet season are subject only to notification. However, inter-basin diversion in the wet season and intra-basin use in the dry season are subject to prior consultation, with inter-basin diversion use during the dry season being subject to prior agreement. Minor domestic uses of water that do not have a significant impact on the mainstream flows were excluded from the 1995 Mekong Agreement.

All three procedural steps (notification, prior consultation, and prior agreement) enable the parties to assess the transboundary impacts of the proposed action on the riparian countries and to mitigate or minimize the harmful effects. In the case of notification, member countries are required to provide additional data and information to allow members to evaluate the impact of the proposed use. Prior consultation is aimed at arriving at an agreement, but it neither provides a veto nor a right of unilateral action. In the most sensitive cases, obtaining specific prior agreement of the JC is necessary.[129]

Through these scoping and procedural mechanisms, constraint on state behaviour and sovereignty is seen to be minimally impaired in the effort to ensure hydrological integrity by preserving at least a certain flow level on the mainstream in varying conditions (Article 6). The objectives of protecting the environment and ecological balance are buttressed by the obligation to prevent (known) harmful effects of uses and reinforcing state responsibility for any damages.[130]

The 1995 Mekong Agreement thus provides a practical opportunity to maximize options for trade-offs, exchanges, or releases from other sources (i.e., lower tributaries from the same riparian country) to protect the flow levels, while optimizing the sharing and use of waters during the dry and wet seasonal variations. In theory, it provides certainty, security, and flexibility to all riparians under what may be termed a 'super-fairness' doctrine.

Article 37 provides that the 1995 Mekong Agreement may be 'amended, modified, superseded or terminated' by the mutual agreement of all parties, thereby contemplating and allowing for flexibility to address future needs.

(e)   Dispute Resolution

In the event that there is a dispute between the parties, the 1995 Mekong Agreement provides four steps in seeking a resolution:

---

129   See 1995 Mekong Agreement, supra note 116, c. II "Definition of Terms."
130   Ibid., arts. 7–8.

1. The MRC has responsibility at first instance for addressing any disagreement, where applicable via the Council (pursuant to Article 18(c)) or via the JC (pursuant to Article 24(f)).
2. If the MRC cannot resolve the dispute at this stage, the issue is to be referred to the respective governments, to be resolved diplomatically (Article 35).
3. If this also proves unsatisfactory, countries may refer the issue to a third party for mediation, such as an international organization, an international professional group, or an individual (Article 35).
4. Finally, countries may refer to international law principles (Article 35).

(f)   Key Initiatives Launched Since the 1995 Mekong Agreement

While the 1995 Mekong Agreement provided a valuable framework to guide the cooperation of the riparian states, much of the provisions were general in nature and would require further action by the MRC to be implemented into practical changes. Notable initiatives that have been put together under the aegis of the MRC over the course of its two plus decades of existence include the following:

1. Agriculture and Irrigation Programme
2. Basin Development Plan Programme
3. Climate Change and Adaptation Initiative
4. Drought Management Programme
5. Environment Programme
6. Fisheries Programme
7. Flood Management & Mitigation Programme
8. Information & Knowledge Management Programme
9. Initiative on Sustainable Hydropower
10. Integrated Capacity Building Programme
11. Mekong Integrated Water Resources Management Project
12. Navigation Programme[131]

Of chief importance is the Basin Development Plan (BDP), the main planning and assessment tool used by the MRC to complement national planning processes for the development of the Basin. The 1995 Mekong Agreement gave the

---

131 *About MRC*, Mekong River Commission, http://www.mrcmekong.org/about-mrc/, accessed July 28, 2016.

JC the responsibility of formulating such plans (under Article 26(b)),[132] with the stated goal of ensuring that Mekong waters and related resources contribute to the sustainable development goals of the riparian states. Poverty reduction was identified as a key objective of these five-year plans, which took a triple bottom line approach in the planning process.

While the first BDP did not commence operation until six years after the conclusion of the 1995 Mekong Agreement, it has since grown to incorporate a number of reinforcing programmes that give effect to the provisions of the 1995 Mekong Agreement. Alongside the first BDP, the MRC initiated the Water Utilization Project (WUP) to realize many of the promises that were made in the BDP. The WUP, which ran from 2000 to 2008, vastly improved the state of basin modelling and knowledge to enable it to support better management decisions going forward. In turn, this aided the implementation of provisions regarding water utilization and strengthened the capacity of the parties to implement the water utilization rules.[133]

Since 2006, the MRC has incorporated integrated water resources management (IWRM) principles into its work. This policy push builds upon the direction that was initiated in the WUP and then carried forward into its strategic plans (2006–2010 and 2011–2015) and then, most prominently, in an IWRM-based BDP in 2011.[134]

In 2010, in collaboration with the private sector, civil society, and other stakeholders, the MRC completed a strategic environmental assessment of the twelve hydropower schemes that are being studied by private sector developers on the Mekong mainstream.[135] Its main conclusion was that decisions on mainstream dams should be deferred for a period of ten years given the limited

---

132 'To formulate a basin development plan, which would be periodically reviewed and revised as necessary; to submit to the Council for approval the basin development plan and joint development projects/programs to be implemented in connection with it; and to confer with donors, directly or through their consultative group, to obtain the financial and technical support necessary for project/program implementation.'

133 For more information on the WUP, see *Projects & Operations: Mekong River Water Utilization Project*, World Bank Group, http://www.worldbank.org/projects/P045864/mekong-river-water-utilization-project?lang=en, accessed July 28, 2016.

134 *Mekong Integrated Water Resources Management Project*, Mekong River Commission, http://www.mrcmekong.org/about-mrc/programmes/mekong-integrated-water-resources-management-project/, accessed July 28, 2016.

135 International Centre for Environmental Management (ICEM), 'Strategic Environmental Assessment of Hydropower on the Mekong Mainstream: Summary of the Final Report,' *ICEM* (2010), http://www.mrcmekong.org/assets/Publications/Consultations/SEA-Hydropower/SEA-FR-summary-13oct.pdf, accessed July 28, 2016.

state of the knowledge of potential impacts and the seriousness of the potential effects on the sensitive environment of the river Basin.[136] However, this conclusion did not get adopted in future BDPs, or otherwise form official MRC policy; in fact, development of hydroelectric dams remained priorities of both Lao PDR and Cambodia going forward.

In addition to these various initiatives, five procedures for the implementation of the MRC framework have been concluded to clarify the obligations of the MRC parties:

1. Procedures for Notification, Prior Consultation and Agreement (PNPCA) (approved in 2003)
2. Procedures for Data and Information Exchange and Sharing (approved in 2001)
3. Procedures for Water Use Monitoring (approved in 2003)
4. Procedures for Maintenance Flows on the Mainstream (approved in 2006)
5. Procedures for Water Quality (approved in 2011)

Of chief importance is the PNPCA, which builds on the 1995 Mekong Agreement to set out in detail the procedures that the parties must follow to communicate the potential impacts of qualifying proposed uses of the Mekong Basin, as well as the responsibilities of the various MRC agencies in this process.[137] In particular, it prescribes that notification must include a feasibility study report, implementation plan, schedule, and all available data. Further guidelines on the implementation of the PNPCA were published in 2005.[138]

Prior consultation also requires the notifying party to provide additional technical data and information, including a summary of the impact assessment documents, to allow the riparians to perform their own proper due diligence with respect to the proposed use. Upon receipt of information, a six-month time period (with option to extend) for consultation begins. Notified States

---

136 Ibid., p. 22.
137 Procedures for Notification, Prior Consultation and Agreement, November 13, 2003, Kingdom of Cambodia, Lao People's Democratic Republic, Kingdom of Thailand, and the Socialist Republic of Viet Nam, http://www.mrcmekong.org/assets/Publications/policies/Procedures-Notification-Prior-Consultation-Agreement.pdf, accessed July 28, 2016.
138 Guidelines on Implementation of the Procedures for Notification, Prior Consultation and Agreement, August 31, 2005, Kingdom of Cambodia, Lao People's Democratic Republic, Kingdom of Thailand, and the Socialist Republic of Viet Nam, http://www.mrcmekong.org/assets/Publications/policies/Guidelines-on-implementation-of-the-PNPCA.pdf, accessed July 28, 2016.

can request further information to aid in their study of the proposed use in this time frame. During this process, the JC aims to arrive at an agreement on the use and potential conditions, and the notifying State is not to commence the proposed use until the other member States have had the ability to discuss and evaluate the proposed use.

Specific agreements need to be approved by all members of the JC, but the form of this agreement is not specified and is, instead, established by the JC on a case-by-case basis. Agreements need to include, among others, the terms and conditions such as timing and quantity of diversion.

III   The Nam Theun 2 Project

The NT2 project was many years in the making before the 1995 Mekong Agreement was finalized. In the preceding years, the Interim Mekong Committee (precursor to the MRC) developed a plan for hydropower development in the Basin, including feasibility studies for the most promising site, NT2. By 1993, a mandate was granted to begin development of NT2. However, it took more than a decade before World Bank and Asian Development Bank-led financing of the project was agreed to and the construction on the US$1.5 billion project began. NT2 was regarded as a key mechanism for increasing regional trade, reducing poverty in Lao PDR, and creating technical know-how in working with the private sector in large PPPs. In turn, the hope was that this would encourage further foreign direct investment (FDI) in the country. The major delays in getting the project off the ground have been summed up as follows:

> NT2 was particularly complicated ... because it was prepared during the challenging times that included the dam debate of the 1990s, which culminated in the World Commission on Dams, the Asian financial crisis of 1997, the strengthening of environmental and social safeguard policies and practices at the World Bank and other financial institutions, and the greater scrutiny of governance arrangements for the transparent use of natural resource rents by countries.[139]

(a)   Context

Lao PDR is described by the World Bank as a lower/middle income country with a population of 6,802,023, with an annual growth of only 1.7%,[140] an annual gross domestic product of US$12 billion, and gross national income (GNI)

---

[139] Porter & Shivakumar, supra note 69, p. 1.
[140] *Population growth (annual %)*, World Bank Group (2015), http://data.worldbank.org/indicator/SP.POP.GROW/countries/LA?display=graph, accessed July 28, 2016.

of US$1,600 (all 2014 numbers).[141] While it has the smallest population and economy of all of the LMRBS, Lao PDR is one of the fastest growing economies in East Asia and the Pacific, averaging a growth rate of 7% over the last decade[142] when the GNI was only US$340.[143] This growth has contributed to a reduction of the percentage of the population living in poverty from 33.5% to 23.2% over that same period. The economy is largely dependent on revenue from natural resource extraction, and infrastructure is largely undeveloped. Corruption remains a key impediment to greater foreign investment; in spite of this, the net annual FDI has increased from US$27,720,000 in 2006 to US$1,079,000,000 in 2015.[144]

Of the 236,000 km^2 area of the country, 97% is in the watershed or catchment area of the Mekong River Basin, with the same percentage of the population residing within the Basin.[145] The country has low urbanization, with about 40% of the population belonging to minority groups settled in the uplands.[146] While the country remains a one-party socialist state, the economy has been rapidly liberalized since the 'New Economic Mechanism' was introduced by the government in 1986.[147]

Increasingly, the export of power to its electricity hungry neighbours has been a major contributor to the rapid growth rate of the country. With an untapped potential of 18,000 MW, and with several large hydro and other power plants currently under construction, this trend is expected to continue.[148] The country is intent on becoming the 'battery of Southeast Asia' and quadrupling its 2014 hydropower generation capacity by 2020.[149] The main market for this power is its western neighbour, Thailand, which is currently exploiting its

---

141 *Lao PDR | Data*, World Bank Group (2015), http://data.worldbank.org/country/lao-pdr?display=graph, accessed July 28, 2016.
142 *Lao PDR Overview*, World Bank Group (2016), http://www.worldbank.org/en/country/lao/overview, accessed July 28, 2016.
143 Sidharth Sinha, 'Nam Theun 2 (NT2) Hydroelectric Project,' *Indian Institute of Management* (2007), p. 2.
144 *Foreign Direct Investment, Net Inflows (BOP, current US$)*, World Bank Group, http://data.worldbank.org/indicator/BX.KLT.DINV.CD.WD?display=graph&locations=LA, accessed July 28, 2016.
145 *Aquastat: Mekong Basin*, Food and Agriculture Organization of the United Nations (2011), http://www.fao.org/nr/water/aquastat/basins/mekong/index.stm, accessed 28 July, 2016.
146 Sinha, supra note 144, p. 2.
147 Porter & Shivakumar, supra note 69, pp. 5–6.
148 *Lao PDR Overview*, supra note 143.
149 F. Tan, 'Laos' Hydropower Generation Capacity to Jump Almost Four-fold by 2020,' *Daily Mail* (October 28, 2014), http://www.dailymail.co.uk/wires/reuters/article-2810681/Laos-hydropower-generation-capacity-jump-four-fold-2020.html, accessed July 28, 2016.

natural gas reserves for a large proportion of its electricity. At this point, Viet Nam is a less developed market for its electricity exports, but it is considered a prime target for such exports in the future. But, with declining reserves, electricity demand rising by 5–6% per year, and environmental constraints on domestic coal and hydro, Thailand has been seeking to further diversify its power supply options.[150]

Plans for large-scale hydropower development throughout the Mekong River Basin have been circulating since the 1950s.[151] The ability to serve its growing domestic power needs while simultaneously carving out an international energy market is seen as a great opportunity for Lao PDR. Lao PDR has been seeking international assistance to finance energy projects, and it has received the support of major development institutions to embark on a major hydropower export and development programme.[152] However, only two large hydroelectric dams had been built before the turn of the century (Nam Ngum I in 1971 and Theun Hinboun in 1998) and before the time the NT2 project attracted the requisite financing to move ahead.[153]

(b)   NT2 Specifications

NT2 is located in the Khammouane and Bolikhamxay provinces in south central Lao PDR, stretching from the Nakai Plateau to the lower Xe Bang Fai River confluence with the Mekong. NT2 is a trans-basin diversion power plant that uses water from the Mekong tributary Nam Theun River and releases the water into another tributary, the Xe Bang Fai River. NT2 stands as a 39-meter-tall and 436-meter long concrete gravity dam, with a 450 km² reservoir. A double-circuit 115 kV transmission line connects the facility to Mahaxai in Lao PDR, and a 138-km long double-circuit 500 kV transmission line connects the facility to the Thai border.[154] The electricity generation capacity of the facility is 1,070 MW of which 995 MW is for export to Thailand and 75 MW for domestic energy needs in Lao PDR.[155]

---

150   *Lao PDR Overview*, supra note 143.
151   Porter & Shivakumar, supra note 69, pp. 2, 9–14.
152   *Lao PDR Overview*, supra note 143.
153   Porter & Shivakumar, supra note 69, pp. 1, 7.
154   *Technical Information*, Nam Theun 2 Power Company, http://www.namtheun2.com/index.php/about-us/techinfo, accessed July 28, 2016.
155   Fleur Johns, On Failing Forward: Neoliberal Legality in the Mekong River Basin,' *Cornell International Law Journal*, Vol. 48(2), pp. 347–383, (2015), p. 355, http://www.lawschool.cornell.edu/research/ILJ/upload/Johns-fnal.pdf, accessed July 28, 2016.

(c)   History

The NT2 site had been identified in the 1980s by the Interim Mekong Committee and was determined to be the most appropriate of the three large dam locations that were then studied.[156] By 1993, a government mandate was received to pursue the development of the dam as a private sector investment project.[157] However, in the coming years, NT2 encountered a number of obstacles that delayed its development, including growing opposition to hydroelectric dams and the 1997 Asian financial crisis (and related slump in electricity demand). The project received extra scrutiny from the World Commission on Dams at a time when the World Bank development strategy was under criticism, particularly with regard to dam development.[158]

As part of the new Water Resources Sector Strategy, the World Bank increasingly focused its efforts on poverty reduction, improving governance and sound environmental and social safety in its criteria for new projects.[159] The World Bank did not commit to funding the project until (1) the Lao PDR government agreed to implement a measurable poverty reduction plan and environmental protection programme, (2) the project met the World Bank safeguard policies and were of an acceptable standard, and (3) broad support of both donors and civil society for both the national development strategy and project was assured.[160]

The aforementioned issues delayed the project until financial closing was finally completed in 2005. That same year construction activities began, and the Nam Theun River was diverted in March of 2006. By 2010 construction activities were completed, and commercial operations began in April of that year.

(d)   Financing and Equity

The project was financed through US$330 million of equity and US$920 million of debt from equity loans and guarantees from MDBs (including the World Bank, ADB, EIB, and the NIB), export credit agencies (COFACE of France, EKN of Sweden, and GIEK of Norway), bilateral financing agencies (French Development Agency, PROPARCO, and the Export-Import Bank of Thailand (Thai Exim Bank)), international commercial banks providing finance in hard currencies (including BNP Paribas, Crédit Agricole Indosuez, ANZ from

---

156   Porter & Shivakumar, supra note 69, p. 2.
157   Ibid.
158   Johns, supra note 156, p. 356.
159   Porter & Shivakumar, supra note 69, p. 11.
160   Ibid., p. 12.

Australia, Société Générale, Fortis Bank, and Bank of Tokyo-Mitsubishi), and Thai commercial banks providing finance in Thai baht.[161]

The project follows a 'Build Own Operate Transfer' PPP framework with a concession period of 31 years (25 of which are operating years) after which the government acquires the rights to the facilities free of charge. The project was developed by the Nam Theun 2 Power Company (NTPC), which is owned by two private consortiums of shareholders, Eléctricité de France (EDF) (40%) and Electricity Generating Public Company Limited (EGCO) of Thailand (35%), with the remaining 25% equity owned by the Lao Holding State Enterprise. The expectation is that the government will receive between US$1.9–2 billion in revenue over the first 25 years of operation, at which point it will receive full ownership rights to the project and the entirety of the revenue it creates[162] (details regarding the financing and contractual structure are set out below).

(e) Impacts

Under the terms of the 1995 Mekong Agreement, considering that NT2 is situated on a tributary rather than the mainstream of the Mekong, Lao PDR was only obliged to notify, rather than undertake prior consultation with, riparian states. The government of Lao PDR issued the required notifications to its riparian neighbours through the MRC Secretariat before commencing construction of the project.[163] Over a decade's worth of consultative, evaluative and supervisory activities implemented by non-governmental organizations (NGOs), development banks, independent panels, and contingent funding provided for ongoing environmental and social programmes would serve to assuage concerns about the negative impacts of the project to a certain extent.

The Lao PDR government undertook an environmental impact assessment of the project. The assessment found that there would be impacts in the form of primary forest and productive agricultural land loss, disruption to wildlife habitats, potential loss of biodiversity, impacts to local fisheries and water, but no significant impacts on protected species or on the Mekong Basin itself.[164]

Several international NGOs led the consultation process of those who would be directly affected by the project. The World Bank put in place an international

---

161 *Shareholders & Financing*, Nam Theun 2 Power Company, http://www.namtheun2.com/index.php/about-us/shareholders, accessed July 28, 2016.
162 Porter & Shivakumar, supra note 69, p. 4.
163 *Update: Nam Theun 2 Hydropower Project, Laos*, European Investment Bank, http://www.eib.org/infocentre/press/news/topical_briefs/2005-november-01/nam-theun-2-hydropower-project-laos.htm, accessed July 28, 2016.
164 Ibid.

advisory group to review the project, in addition to the monitoring and advisory roles that would typically be associated with such a project. Two independent expert panels were formed to monitor for environmental and social impacts, and for dam safety as part of the Concession Agreement.

The project sought to generate a diverse suite of environmental and social benefits through directed funding for beneficial programmes. These programmes included new conservation measures to reduce threats to forest resources; the establishment of long-term watershed protection and management systems for the Nakai Nam Theun National Protected Area and associated corridors; compensatory forest protection to offset the loss of primary forest in the reservoir; the establishment of resettlement villages and farms and compensation for livelihood losses, and the creation of livelihood development initiatives for people who would be forced to resettle as a result from the river diversion; and creating reservoir fisheries management by local people, with extensive independent monitoring, including penalties for non-compliance.[165] Further, the project provided funding to strengthen revenue and expenditure management in Lao PDR, including a specific directive and the establishment of a fund to ensure that revenue from the project was exclusively directed to poverty reduction efforts.[166]

(f)   Significance

The NT2 project has been an impactful project both from an economic standpoint and from a capacity building perspective. The project was undertaken in a very challenging economic political and environmental setting. There was extra pressure in that the eventual outcome would be symbolic in determining future World Bank investments worldwide. Regionally, it provided a test of the MRC notification process for a project that had the potential for the regional sharing of benefits from the Basin's resources. Nationally, the project has been referred to as 'an essential part of the country's development framework' and the project's implementation 'is likely to be the first real possibility for [Lao PDR] to reduce gradually its dependence on Official Development Assistance.'[167] It also provided a case study for large-scale foreign investment in Lao PDR and indicates the extent of its transition to a market-based economy.

The project is responsible for a variety of important legal reforms, including changes in public administration, investment, property, natural resources, and

---

165   Ibid.
166   Johns, supra note 156, p. 357.
167   *Project in Brief*, Nam Theun 2 Power Company, http://www.namtheun2.com/index.php/about-us/project-in-brief, accessed July 28, 2016.

environmental protection.[168] By November, 2015, five years into operations, major tangible benefits had been realized, including over US$174 million in revenues from the project, US$65 million spent towards successfully resettling over 6,000 people in 1,300 new and vastly improved homes, construction of over 120 km of all-weather access roads, 16 nursery and 17 primary schools, two health centres and an upgraded hospital, and community infrastructure. Significant efforts and financing were directed to strengthen re-settler livelihoods through the provision of new equipment, advisory services and vocational training.[169] The project has also met its energy production targets and has served as a key cog in the nation's strategy to become the 'battery of Southeast Asia.'

However, the extensive programmes, environmental monitoring and safeguards present in the NT2 project have not been standardized in subsequent hydroelectric projects on the Mekong. The mainstream Xayaburi dam, another PPP hydropower project that is currently under construction, but without the involvement of the ADB or World Bank, did not elicit the same framework. Notably, the engagement with NGOs was lacking, public consultation was at best limited, funding for similar environmental programmes and monitoring and independent assessments were not present, nor was specific funding earmarked for legal reforms or guarantees made that revenues would be directed to poverty reduction efforts. The Lao PDR government was convinced that the experience of the NT2 project had made such programmes superfluous, and that it would therefore modify the terms in its project and concession agreement to omit these commitments. Details of the Xayaburi project will be discussed in Chapter Eight.

E   Contractual Structure

A large-scale transnational infrastructure project such as NT2 is constructed on the basis of a complex and interconnected web of contracts that assign rights, obligations, and risk to the various parties to the PPP.[170] This web of connected contracts requires the cohesive interplay of various rights and obligations to bring the project to fruition and, ultimately, to operation. Central to each project is usually a PPP contract, such as a concession agreement or similar

---

168   Johns, supra note 156, pp. 357–358.
169   'Statement on the Release of the NT2 Panel of Experts 24th Report,' *World Bank Group* (November 9, 2015), http://www.worldbank.org/en/news/press-release/2015/11/05/statement-on-the-release-of-the-nt2-panel-of-experts-24th-report, accessed July 28, 2016.
170   Rondon, supra note 19, pp. 74–79.

document, between the public (granting) authority and the private partner.[171] A significant feature of PPPs is the mobilization of private capital and expertise. This greater role of private capital and parties also means a greater risk allocation to the private sector in these infrastructure projects. To create this particular relationship and to allocate the respective risks, the contractual terms and structure of a PPP deal is of central importance. 'State ownership or custodianship of water resources is gradually emerging as the rule.'[172] As such, a concession contract between the governing state authority and the private actor in the PPP is a pivotal document for a large-scale infrastructure project such as NT2.

This section will outline some of the relevant contractual forms and terms associated with an infrastructure PPP project such as NT2, while providing links for further reading. It will also provide a brief overview of the contractual makeup of NT2. However, due to the constraints of space, this section will not provide an exhaustive discussion of all the contractual structures available to large-scale infrastructure projects or the international and domestic law that would pertain to such contracts.

I   *PPP Contractual Structure*

PPPs are a particular type of contractual regime, though not all are composed of the same contractual parts. In this section, we will identify a few contractual terms common to large-scale hydropower projects, such as NT2, to set up as a PPP.

The concession agreement[173] is the contract by which the public party grants the right to use a government resource or asset to the private party, or

---

171   'Report on Recommended PPP Contractual Provisions,' 2015 Edition, *World Bank Group* (2015), p. 6, http://ppp.worldbank.org/public-private-partnership/sites/ppp.worldbank.org/files/ppp_testdumb/documents/150808_wbg_report_on_recommended_ppp_contractual_provisions.pdf, accessed August 5, 2016.

172   'Yet exceptions are allowed in some countries for some form of private ownership.' Salman Salman & Daniel Bradlow, 'Regulatory Frameworks for Water Resources Management: A Comparative Study,' Law, Justice, and Development Series No. 36216, *World Bank Group*, (2006), p. 164, http://web.worldbank.org/archive/website01021/WEB/IMAGES/362160RE.PDF, accessed August 1, 2016.

173   'Some terms such as Concessions and Affermage have a definite technical meaning and structure to them in certain civil law jurisdictions that may not be understood or applied in a common law country. Care should be taken, therefore, in applying these terms loosely.' *Key Features of Common Law or Civil Law Systems*, World Bank Group, Public-Private-Partnership in Infrastructure Resource Center, http://ppp.worldbank.org/public-private-partnership/legislation-regulation/framework-assessment/legal-systems/common-vs-civil-law, accessed August 2, 2016.

allows the provision of a public service for a specified period.¹⁷⁴ With respect to infrastructure, the concession typically grants responsibility for operations, maintenance, and some investment.

The power purchase agreement (PPA), which is sometimes referred to as an offtake agreement, governs the sale and purchase of the power generated by a project between a seller/producer and an offtaker (usually a public utility).¹⁷⁵ The PPA is essential for providing certainty to the private partner(s) that they will receive a reliable return for the provision of power from the operation of the project to cover its costs, as well as provide a reasonable return on its shareholder investment. For the offtaker it secures a specific amount of power from the producer.

It is obviously of vital importance that the various components of a contract relate to each other. In large infrastructure projects such as NT2, which comprise several contracts, it is important that these interlocking contracts be compatible with each other.

Some countries have sought to standardize PPP contractual terms and elements of design, or have sought to create model contracts, or at least standardize specific sections of PPP contracts through legislation.¹⁷⁶ There are sector specific, national and international resources and initiatives to standardize 'concession law' or PPP contract law.¹⁷⁷ These efforts reflect a desire to streamline the significant time and costs often associated with the development and negotiation of elaborate contractual structures.¹⁷⁸ The World Bank notes:

> [T]here is no universally-accepted language for such agreements on an international basis. Given the variety of PPP transactions globally, the

---

174 *Concessions, Build-Operate-Transfer (BOT) and Design-Build-Operate (DBO) Projects*, World Bank Group, Public-Private-Partnership in Infrastructure Resource Center, http://ppp.worldbank.org/public-private-partnership/agreements/concessions-bots-dbos, accessed August 2, 2016.

175 Mohammed Badissy et al., 'Understanding Power Purchase Agreements,' Vol. 1.3, *United States Department of Commerce, Commercial Law Development Program* (2014), p. 24, http://cldp.doc.gov/sites/default/files/Understanding_Power_Purchase_Agreements.pdf, accessed July 29, 2016.

176 'For example, Chile has established PPP the dispute resolution mechanism in its concession law.' Public-Private Partnerships Reference Guide, supra note 3, p. 157.

177 *Standardized Agreements, Bidding Documents and Guidance Manuals*, World Bank Group, Public-Private-Partnership in Infrastructure Resource Center (2016), http://ppp.worldbank.org/public-private-partnership/standardized-agreements-bidding-documents-and-guidance-manuals#Standardized%20PPP%20Contracts, accessed August 3, 2016.

178 Report on Recommended PPP Contractual Provisions, supra note 172, p. 6.

different legal systems which exist in various countries, and the need to have 'tailor-made' provisions to deal with the individual characteristics of specific projects, it follows that the development of comprehensive PPP agreements on an international basis is likely an unrealistic goal. However, there may be merit in focusing on certain contractual provisions dealing with particular legal issues encountered in virtually every PPP contract, such as the issues of force majeure, termination rights, dispute resolution, etc.[179]

It is important to assess the law of the host nation to establish if the contractual terms and objectives of the PPP are permissible and enforceable within that jurisdiction.[180] In particular, there are distinct differences between contracting within a civil law and a common law system that need to be taken into account.[181] It is therefore very important to obtain local legal advice and to develop a familiarity with the relevant domestic legal system.

II   Key Elements

Successful concession contracts clearly delineate the respective rights and obligations of the contracting parties along with clear performance and development targets, while building in appropriate provisions to provide flexibility for unforeseen circumstances and possible termination. Sufficient means of ensuring ongoing monitoring and management of performance targets and standards should be incorporated into the concession contract. The World Bank Group's reference guide on PPPs identifies five key areas of PPP contract design[182] that collectively outline the risk allocation under the contract:

---

179   Ibid., p. 6.
180   See *Legal and Regulatory Issues Concerning Public-Private Partnerships*, World Bank Group, Public-Private-Partnership in Infrastructure Resource Center, http://ppp.worldbank.org/public-private-partnership/legislation-regulation, accessed July 29, 2016; *PPP Knowledge Lab—Countries*, World Bank Group, Public-Private-Partnership in Infrastructure Resource Center, https://pppknowledgelab.org/countries, accessed July 29, 2016.
181   A civil system is generally more prescriptive and will have more implied provisions requiring generally shorter contracts and reducing the need to fully define all of the contractual terms. See *Key Features of Common Law or Civil Law Systems*, supra note 173.
182   For further reading on PPPs, including a selection of sample PPP contracts and agreements as well as a wealth of other PPP related tools, see *Public-Private-Partnership in Infrastructure Resource Center*, World Bank Group, http://ppp.worldbank.org/ppp/, accessed July 29, 2016. See also Badissy et al., supra note 176.

1. **Performance requirements**—defining the required quality and quantity of assets and services, along with monitoring and enforcement mechanisms, including penalties.
2. **Payment mechanisms**—defining how the private party will be paid, through user charges, government payments based on usage or availability, or a combination, and how bonuses and penalties can be built in.
3. **Adjustment mechanisms**—building in to the contract mechanisms for handling changes, such as extraordinary reviews of tariffs, or changing service requirements.
4. **Dispute resolution procedures**—defining institutional mechanisms for how contractual disputes will be resolved, such as the role of the regulator and courts, or the use of expert panels or international arbitration.
5. **Termination provisions**—defining the contract term, handover provisions, and circumstances and implications of early termination.[183]

III *The Nam Theun 2 Hydropower Project*

The construction and operation of NT2[184] is built on a myriad of interdependent contracts, all of which cannot be mentioned here.[185] It is important to discuss the concession agreement between Lao PDR and NTPC, the most critical component of the PPP contracts. NT2 is structured as a build-own-operate-transfer (BOOT) project, where NTPC is responsible for developing, owning, financing, constructing, and operating the hydroelectric plant and related facilities.[186] The concession agreement specifies a 25-year period, starting from the commercial operations date, during which NTPC holds such rights.[187] After that period elapses, the project will be transferred back to the Government of Lao, at no cost.[188]

---

183 Public-Private Partnerships Reference Guide, supra note 3, p. 157.
184 See Nam Theun 2 Power Company Limited, 'Nam Theun 2 Hydroelectric Project, Summary of the Concession Agreement between The Government of the Lao PDR and Nam Theun 2 Power Company, as of November, 2005,' http://siteresources.worldbank.org/INTLAOPRD/Resources/293582-1092106399982/492430-1092106479653/SummaryofCA.pdf, accessed August 4, 2016.
185 For example, some of these contracts include the head construction contract, the sponsors' agreement, and the shareholders' agreement.
186 Nam Theun 2 Power Company Limited, supra note 185, p. 2.
187 'Hydropower in Asia: The Nam Theun 2 Project,' *World Bank Group, Multilateral Investment Guarantee Agency* (2006), p. 3, https://www.miga.org/documents/NT206.pdf, accessed July 28, 2016.
188 Porter & Shivakumar, supra note 69, p. 4.

The electricity produced by the facility will be sold under two separate 'take-or-pay' PPAs, one with Electricity Generating Authority of Thailand (EGAT) and the other with Electricité du Lao (EDL), Lao's state-owned power company. The EGAT PPA, signed between EGAT and NTPC in 2003, is for NTPC to provide up to 995 MW of generating capacity, and is valid for 25 years from the commercial operations date.[189] The EDL PPA, also signed in 2003 for a 25-year period, contracts NTPC to provide 75 MW of generating capacity.[190]

World Bank experts provided guidance regarding contract design, including support to the government on the development of the PPA and concession agreements. World Bank staff were directly involved in supporting the development of schedule 4 of the concession agreement which deals with safeguards.[191] 'A budget of [US]$20 million was allocated for breach of concession agreement obligations and unanticipated impacts, including for the downstream area … the concession agreement contains clear financial provisions to ensure that environmental and social obligations are met.'[192]

The NT2 PPP is thus reflective of the typical contracts that govern PPP infrastructure projects, such as concession agreements and PPAs. The NT2 concession agreement is notable for including specific environmental and social mitigation measures that need to be undertaken by both NTPC and the Lao PDR government, and which are discussed in both the preceding and following sections. In order to provide a product for two distinct national markets, two PPAs were required. The lynchpin to convince the private sector to invest were the risk guarantees that were provided by a number of MDBs. These guarantees are discussed immediately below.

F   Project Cost and Financing/Risk Mitigation

In the early to mid-1990s, the impetus for developing NT2 came from the private sector and the financing was sought from commercial banks. However, because of risks associated with dam construction and uncertainties about the political commitment and governance capacity of the Lao PDR government, commercial banks sought additional insurance from an international financial institution before making such a sizable investment.

---

189   Hydropower in Asia, supra note 188, p. 2.
190   Porter & Shivakumar, supra note 69, p. 149.
191   Ibid., p. 95.
192   Ibid., p. 67.

The ADB was reluctant to participate because of its overexposure in Lao PDR. Both the government and the developers were initially reluctant to approach the World Bank, thinking that the stringent requirements and conditions would slow progress and make the project financially impractical, but there were no other feasible options available.[193] The World Bank was therefore approached and conducted a series of studies and a technical review of the project, beginning in 1995. Subsequent delays in getting guarantees led to then lead developer, Transfield, and two Thai companies that were involved in the initial consortium selling their shares to the new lead developer, EDF, and to EGCO, respectively.[194]

Apart from low-level bridging activities undertaken by the Bank, the Asian financial crisis effectively caused the project to stall until 2001.[195] By that point, the regional financial situation had largely stabilized and the project took on a new life with some changes in the developer group and a more complicated decision-making framework.[196] A new focus on mitigating environmental and social impacts, and ensuring proceeds were directed to poverty reduction (outlined above), attracted other multilateral donors and financiers, including the ADB, Agence Française de Développement (AFD), EIB, NIB, and a host of private financiers that were comfortable that many of the risks had been mitigated.[197]

I Project Cost

Having only recently transitioned to a market-based economy, Lao PDR faces major domestic resource constraints on financing development. As such, it has focused on promoting private sector involvement to realize its development goals.[198] The prospect of financing a project of the magnitude of NT2 was a great challenge from the onset and became even more so with the additional safeguard policies and associated costs that needed to be satisfied for the involvement of multilateral financial institutions. The base cost estimate of NT2 amounted to US$1.25 billion, and the development group earmarked

---

193 Ibid., p. 10.
194 Ibid.
195 Ibid., p. 11.
196 Ibid., p. 99.
197 Ibid., pp. 11–12.
198 W. Um et al., 'Report and Recommendation of the President to the Board of Directors on a Proposed Loan to the Lao People's Democratic Republic for the Greater Mekong Subregion: Nam Theun 2 Hydroelectric Project,' *Asian Development Bank* (2005), p. 3.

Summary of Project Base Cost Estimates ($ million)

Item	Foreign Exchange	Local Currency	Total
A. Construction Cost	396.2	315.3	711.5
B. Environmental/Social Mitigation	48.8	0.0	48.8
C. Development Cost	150.6	14.0	164.6
D. Financing Cost	173.0	106.3	279.3
E. Base Contingencies	27.1	18.7	45.8
Total Base Cost	**795.7**	**454.3**	**1,250.0**
Total contingent costs	116.6	83.4	200
Total	**912.3**	**537.7**	**1,450.0**

FIGURE 4   *Nam Theun 2, summary of project base cost estimates.*

an additional US$200 million for contingent costs, bringing the total to US$1.45 billion. Figure 4 represents a summary of the project costs.[199]

II   Project Capital Structure

In order the meet the high cost of the project, a split of 28% equity (US$350 million) and 72% by debt (US$900 million) was settled on. A ratio of 50% equity and 50% debt was chosen to finance the US$200 million contingent costs. A mix of dollars and baht was settled on to match the currency composition of the project base costs, and a 50/50 mix of such currencies was chosen to match the tariff to be paid to the developers and to reduce the mismatch of revenues received by the NTPC and the amounts that it needed to pay its lenders.

The prospect of raising sufficient commercial debt to finance a large, complex infrastructure project in a small poor country with limited creditworthiness was a daunting challenge.[200] Seeking private capital was also a new and politically contentious notion for Lao PDR, which had little experience in this regard.[201] NT2 also represented the first major cross-border hydropower project on the Mekong River (and in the nascent MRC), as well as in Southeast Asia as a whole.

III   Mitigating Risks

The due diligence work of the World Bank and other international financial institutions was critical in bringing along other partners, particularly those which assuaged social, environmental, and revenue management concerns.

---

199   Ibid., p. 14.
200   Porter & Shivakumar, supra note 69, p. 81.
201   Ibid., p. 137.

For example, it was not until 2003 that ADB and AFD joined the project, while MIGA did not join until 2004. These and other official agencies such as EIB, NIB, the Guarantee Institute for Export Credits (GIEK), COFACE, Proparco, Exportkreditnamnden (EKN), and the Thai Exim Bank were able to step in at a later date with a good sense of how the risks of the project could be mitigated.[202] The project financing was structured as a limited recourse financing where the completion risk is allocated to NTPC and its contractors dependent on the actor that is responsible for specific project activities.[203]

Coordinating support from the various international institutions and commercial lenders proved to be a tricky process, requiring a harmonization of policies, procedures, and safeguards. To accomplish this, a single common set of principles was applied. This meant that a default by NTPC on environmental and social matters would lead to a default on all the commercial, bilateral, and multilateral components of the financing package.[204] Similarly, COFACE negotiated an 'export credit policy' with the developers that was followed by GIEK and EKN, obviating the need to negotiate separate agreements with each of the export credit agencies.[205]

IV *Political Risk Guarantees*

Political risk mitigation instruments[206] were used as part of the financing package. These mechanisms were a relatively novel instrument at the time, but were seen by the World Bank and international commercial banks as the only practical option and critical precursor to mobilize sufficient private capital to fund such a project.[207] NTPC and the Lao PDR government thus approached IDA and MIGA of the World Bank and ADB to provide insurance in the international lending package for the project.

After a significant amount of due diligence on the merits and risks of the project were concluded, IDA, MIGA, and ADB settled on providing a mix of

---

202 Ibid., p. 83.
203 Sinha, supra note 144, p. 10.
204 Porter & Shivakumar, supra note 69, p. 83.
205 Ibid., pp. 83–84.
206 'Risk mitigation instruments are financial instruments that transfer certain defined risks from project financiers (lenders and equity investors) to creditworthy third parties (guarantors and insurers) that have a better capacity to accept such risks.' See Tomoko Matsukawa & Odo Habeck, 'Review of Risk Mitigation Instruments for Infrastructure Financing and Recent Trends and Developments,' *Public Private Infrastructure Advisory Facility of the World Bank* (2007), p. xi, https://openknowledge.worldbank.org/bitstream/handle/10986/6778/405300Riskomit101OFFICIAL0USE0ONLY1.pdf?sequence=1&isAllowed=y, accessed July 28, 2016.
207 Hydropower in Asia, supra note 188, p. 3.

guarantees for the project. This would become the first time IDA provided a guarantee in support of hydropower development as well as the first project to use a mix of IDA, MIGA, and ADB guarantees.[208] These guarantees included a total of US$42 million from each of the three respective bodies and would serve as the basis to provide the necessary reassurance for the international commercial banks.

The IDA partial risk guarantee covered a syndicated commercial loan to NTPC that would insure any debt service default that came as a result of activities of the Lao PDR government such as expropriation, changes in law, and other obligations defined in the concession agreement and related agreements that are outside of NTPC control.[209] A fee of 2% per annum was charged to NTPC, of which 0.75% was to be paid to IDA and 1.25% to the Lao PDR government, as long as the government was not responsible for any default.

MIGA provided political risk guarantees to the international dollar lenders of the project to cover non-shareholder loans and related interest thereon to NTPC for a period of 20 years. The guarantees cover the risks of expropriation, breach of contract, transfer restriction, war, and civil disturbance in Lao PDR, and breach of contract, transfer restriction and war/civil disturbance in Thailand as well.[210] Fortis Bank NV of Belgium and Electricité de France International (EdFI) are the main beneficiaries of the guarantees, receiving coverage of up to 97.5% of non-shareholder loans and up to 90% of the equity. Finally, the ADB partial risk guarantee covers against both Thai and Lao political risks.

With the risk guarantees provided by the ABD, MIGA, and IDA, the project was able to involve a variety of multilateral and bilateral financial institutions. A total of US$326 million of international lending was covered by guarantees (including the US$200 million covered by export credit agencies COFACE of France, EKN of Sweden and GIEK of Norway). Supplementing these guarantees, direct loans from a number of multilateral and bilateral development agencies were provided, including from ADB, NIB, AFD, PROPARCO, and the Thai Exim Bank.

These risk mitigation efforts were sufficient to encourage the private sector to get involved in the financing of the project. Nine international commercial banks (ANZ, BNP Paribas, BOTM, Calyon, Fortis Bank, ING, KBC, SG, and Standard Chartered) and seven Thai commercial banks (Bangkok Bank, Bank of Ayudhya, Kasikorn Bank, Krung Thai Bank, Siam City Bank, Siam Commercial Bank, and Thai Military Bank) agreed to provide long-term loans

---

208 Porter & Shivakumar, supra note 69, p. 82.
209 Sinha, supra note 144, pp. 10–11. See also Porter & Shivakumar, supra note 69, p. 84.
210 Sinha, supra note 144, p. 11.

to NTPC.[211] A total of US$326 million was provided by these banks, who participated as a 'club deal,' eliminating duplication of due diligence tasks, and making discussions and negotiations relatively smooth for such a large group of actors.[212] Figure 5 sets out the details of the financing plan.

NT2 Final Project Financing Plan

Source of financing	Amount of financing		Total financing (dollars at exchange rate of 40.1 baht per dollar)
	Millions of dollars	Millions of Thai baht	
Export credit agency facility	200.0		200.0
CoFACE (France)	136.0		136.0
EKN (Sweden)	29.0		29.0
GIEK (Norway)	35.0		35.0
IDA political risk guarantee facility	42.0		42.0
ADB ordinary capital resources facility	50.0		50.0
ADB political risk guarantee facility	42.0		42.0
MIGA political risk guarantee facility	42.0		42.0
AFD facility	30.0		30.0
NIB facility	34.0		34.0
Proparco facility	30.0		30.0
Thai Exim facility	30.0		30.0
Commercial bank facility		20,000.0	500.0
Total long-term debt	500.0	20,000.0	1,000.0
Tranche A	450.0	18,000.0	900.0
Tranche B	50.0	2,000.0	100.0
Total equity	445.2	190.5	450.0
Tranche A	345.2	190.5	350.0
Tranche B	100.0		100.0
Private equity	332.7	190.5	337.5
Government equity	112.5		112.5
ADB loan	16.1		
AFD grant	6.2		
EIB loan	41.0		
IDA grant	20.0		
Government contribution	29.2		
Total base and contingent financing	945.2	20,190.5	1,450.0

FIGURE 5   *Nam Theun 2 final project financing plan.*

---

211 Ibid., p. 10.
212 Porter & Shivakumar, supra note 69, p. 84.

The equity in NT2 breaks down as follows: EdFI, 35 percent; the Italian Thai Development Public Company, 15 percent; EGCO, 25 percent; and the Lao PDR government, 25 percent. The US$350 million investment is shared pro rata by NTPC's four shareholders. In order to fund the government equity injections, an innovative package of loans, credits, and grants was put together by IDA, AFD, EIB, and ADB.[213] In total, these organizations contributed via direct loans to the Lao PDR government in the amount of US$83.3 million to assist the government in financing its equity contribution.[214] US$20 million of this figure represents an IDA grant that funds the Nam Theun 2 Social and Environment Project (NTSEP), which oversees the management of the social and environmental impacts and independent monitoring and evaluation of the NT2 project.[215] Figure 6 depicts the debt and equity financing plan.[216]

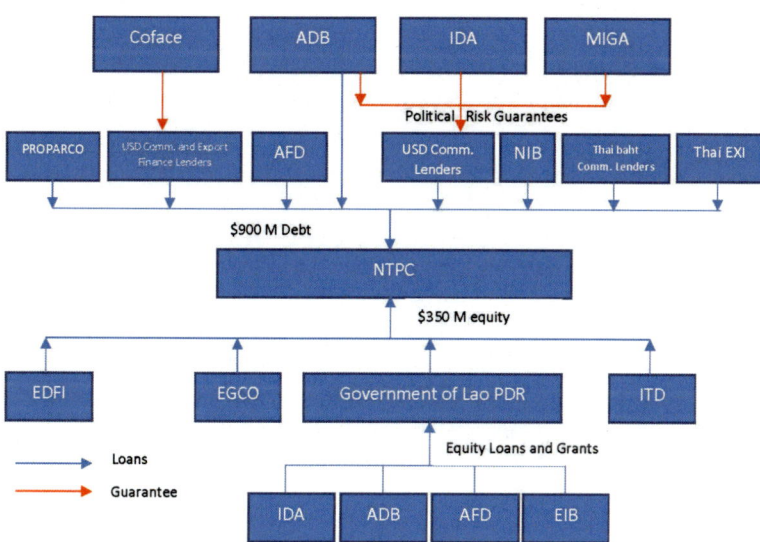

FIGURE 6   *Nam Theun 2 debt and equity financing plan.*

---

213 The ADB's OCR loan has a 30-year term, including a grace period of six years to match the construction period of 4.5 years and first year of commercial operation. See Um et al., supra note 199, p. 16.
214 Porter & Shivakumar, supra note 69, p. 82.
215 Ibid., p. 14.
216 Um et al., supra note 199, p. 15.

On March 31, 2005, the World Bank's Board approved the financing plan for NT2, and several days later, on April 5, 2005, the ADB's Board and the other partners followed suit.[217] Through an innovative use of political risk guarantees and loans to finance the Lao PDR equity in the project, a relatively small amount of public resources were able to leverage about US$1.15 billion of limited recourse private funding through shareholders' equity and long-term private commercial bank debt for NT2.[218]

NT2 began commercial operations in April of 2010, with only a four-month delay from the original schedule, and with a relatively slight base cost overrun of around US$40 million.[219] These additional costs fell well within the expected US$200 million in contingencies and represent low numbers for a project involving US$1.25 billion of capital, and whose construction proceeded over 54 months.

The successful financing of the US$1.45 billion NT2 was no small feat. The project partners had to overcome the limited creditworthiness of Lao PDR, work with a variety of multilateral and bilateral institutions (and respective safeguard policies), finance in multiple currencies, secure guarantees from the World Bank, ADB, and several export credit agencies, and secure loans from 16 different banks, all of which took place in the wake of the Asian financial crisis and at a time where hydroelectric projects were being highly scrutinized.

Until the conclusion of the US$2.6 billion Xayaburi Dam financing (as described in Part G below), NT2 was the largest foreign investment ever made in Lao PDR. At the time financing was finalized, NT2 represented the world's largest private cross-border hydropower financing venture and one of the largest internationally-financed independent power generation projects in Asia since the financial crisis of the late 1990s.[220]

The process of financing NT2 has provided invaluable experience and exposure to Lao PDR, vastly improving its prospects as a recipient of future foreign direct investment. It has further increased its creditworthiness such that potential international lenders and private developers would seriously consider taking risk for future projects in Lao PDR without the sort of multilateral guarantees that were employed in NT2.[221] Several cross-border energy projects have already been proposed and have since commenced without the involvement of multilateral institutions.

---

217   Porter & Shivakumar, supra note 69, p. 14.
218   Sinha, supra note 144, p. 9.
219   Porter & Shivakumar, supra note 69, p. 164.
220   Ibid., p. 14.
221   Ibid., p. 138.

While complex, an NT2-like financial package with multilateral guarantee instruments should be strongly considered for countries that are seeking to develop large complex infrastructure projects when faced with limited public resources and creditworthiness.[222] However, it should be noted that the NT2 package was possible only as a result of a suite of distinct and favourable conditions, including the involvement of a very reputable international company EDF, the favorable economics of NT2, the existing regional understandings on water and power, and a creditworthy off-taker (EGAT).[223] An NT2 finance model may thus have to be modified and adapted where some or all of these factors are less pronounced.

G   Xayaburi Project

The Xayaburi hydroelectric power project provides interesting comparisons and contrasts to NT2, as a subsequent hydroelectric PPP project built in Laos on the Mekong River just a few years after NT2 began operations. As will be described below, Xayaburi has drawn a much more negative response apparently due to both domestic and transboundary environmental and social impacts. The Xayaburi experience also raises the issue of whether the MRC will be an effective forum to manage the Mekong River going forward.

In comparison with the NT2 project, Xayaburi in many ways presented a far bigger challenge. For example, Xayaburi is more expensive (US$3.8 billion to US$1.45 billion), has a more streamlined legal and financial structure, and is more complex because being located on the mainstream of the Mekong River rather than on a tributary necessitates intricate design features to minimize downstream impacts.[224] There are a large number of references in the scholarly, academic, and popular literature to the Xayaburi project.[225]

---

222   Ibid., p. 82.
223   Ibid., p. 138.
224   'Background Material on Pöyry's Assignment,' *Pöyry* (2012), p. 8, http://www.poyry.com/sites/default/files/imce/eng_xayaburi_hpp_09112012_final.pdf, accessed July 19, 2016.
225   See, for example, Johns, supra note 156; Jian Ke & Qi Gao, 'Only One Mekong: Developing Transboundary EIA Proceedures of Mekong River Basin,' *Pace Environmental Law Review*, Vol. 30(3), pp. 950–1004 (2013); Scott C. Armstrong, 'Water is for Fighting: Transnational Legal Disputes in the Mekong River Basin,' *Vermont Journal of Environmental Law*, Vol. 17(1), pp. 1–26 (2015); Frank Lawson,'Sustainable Development Along International Watercourses: Is Progress Being Made?,' *University of Denver Water Law Review*, Vol. 16(2), pp. 323–348 (2013); Sara Vinson et al., 'International Environmental Law: The Year in Review,' *American Bar Association*, Vol. 48, pp. 435–452 (2014), http://www.americanbar

The World Bank and ADB, and the wide-ranging social and environmental safeguards agenda that they were so influential in creating for NT2 are relatively absent from the Xayaburi project's financing. Instead, Xayaburi was financed

.org/content/dam/aba/uncategorized/international_law/environmental.authcheck dam.pdf, accessed June 24, 2016; Bernadette Maheandiran, 'Calling for Clarity: How Uncertainty Undermines the Legitimacy of the Dispute Resolution System under the OECD Guidelines for Multinational Enterprises,' *Harvard Negotiation Law Review*, Vol. 20, pp. 205–244 (2015); Alistair Rieu-Clarke, 'Notification and Consultation Procedures Under the Mekong Agreement: Insights from the Xayaburi Controversy,' *Asian Journal of International Law*, Vol. 5(1), pp. 143–175 (2015); Claudia Kuenzer et al., 'Understanding the Impact of Hydropower Developments in the Context of Upstream-Downstream Relations in the Mekong River Basin,' *Sustainability Science*, Vol. 8(4), pp. 565–584 (2013); Dan Tarlock, 'Toward a More Robust International Water Law of Cooperation to Address Droughts and Ecosystem Conservation,' *Georgetown Environmental Law Review*, Vol. 28(2), pp. 261–290 (2016); 'The Mekong River: Lies, Dams and Statistics: Xayaburi and Vientiane,' *The Economist* (April 26, 2012), http://www.economist.com/blogs/banyan/2012/07/mekong-river, accessed July 19, 2016; Marc Goichot, 'Multiple Dams are an Ominous Threat to Life on the Mekong River,' *The Guardian* (May 6, 2015), https://www.theguardian.com/sustainable-business/2015/may/06/dams-hydropower-mekong-river-thailand-laos-don-sahong-xayaburi, accessed July 19, 2016; *Xayaburi Hydroelectric Power Project*, Ch. Karnchang Public Company Limited, http://www.ch-karnchang.co.th/en/#/project/detail/112/energy-xayaburi-hydroelectric-power-project, accessed July 19, 2016; 'CK Gets B19bn environmental contracts for Xayaburi Dam,' *Bangkok Post* (May 18, 2016), http://www.bangkokpost.com/news/asean/978185/ck-gets-b19bn-environmental-contract-for-xayaburi-dam, accessed July 19, 2016; 'Construction Forges Ahead at Xayaburi Dam,' *Bangkok Post* (July 22, 2012), accessed July 19, 2016; Jonah Fisher, 'Laos Approves Xayaburi 'Mega' Dam on Mekong,' *British Broadcasting Corporation* (November 6, 2012), http://www.bbc.com/news/world-asia-20203072, accessed July 19, 2016; 'Thai State Agencies Likely to Get Away with Xayaburi Dam Construction,' *Prachatai English* (November 30, 2015), http://www.prachatai.com/english/node/5650, accessed July 19, 2016; Martin Petty, 'Laos Defies Neighbours on Dam Project—Environmentalists,' *Reuters* (June 23, 2011), http://www.reuters.com/article/laos-dam-idUSL3E7HN1L320110623, accessed July 19, 2016; Joshua Kurlantzick, 'In Southeast Asia, Big Dams Raise Big Concerns,' *Council on Foreign Relations* (June 30, 2011), http://blogs.cfr.org/asia/2011/06/30/in-southeast-asia-big-dams-raise-big-concerns/, accessed July 19, 2016; 'Xayaburi Dam Building Pact Signed,' *Eco-Business* (April 17, 2012), http://www.eco-business.com/news/xayaburi-dam-building-pact-signed/, accessed July 19, 2016; *Xayaburi Power Company Limited: Private Company Information*, Bloomberg, http://www.bloomberg.com/research/stocks/private/snapshot.asp?privcapid=113025177, accessed July 19, 2016; 'Substandard Dam Assessment Opens Way to Fisheries Destruction on Mekong,' *World Wildlife Fund*, (April 14, 2011), http://wwf.panda.org/wwf_news/press_releases/?200016/Substandard-dam-assessment-opens-way-to-fisheries-destruction-on-Mekong, accessed July 19, 2016.

largely by debt raised from various Thai commercial banks (one of them state-owned) and the Thai Exim Bank.[226]

Xayaburi is located on the mainstream of the Mekong River, in the northern Lao PDR province of Xayaburi, approximately 80 kilometres south of Luang Prabang.[227] The project is designed as a 32.6-meter high, 820-meter long concrete gravity dam located on the mainstream of the Mekong River.[228] Significantly, Xayaburi will be the first hydroelectric dam to be constructed outside of China on the main stem of the Mekong River. Xayaburi includes the development of a 1,285 MW power plant that will export approximately 1,225 MW of electricity to Thailand under a take-or-pay PPA with the Thai state-owned EGAT, and will supply about 60 MW to the Laos PDR state-owned EDL for domestic consumption.[229] The project is expected to be complete and in commercial operation in 2019.[230]

The special purpose corporate vehicle created for the Xayaburi project is Xayaburi Power Company Limited (XPC). Like NT2, Xayaburi is a BOOT project where XPC is the beneficiary of a 29-year concession from Lao PDR, with the entitlement to build, own, and operate and then transfer it back to the state at the end of the concession term.[231] XPC is a

> limited liability company created under Lao PDR law and is fifty percent owned by Ch. Karnchang Public Company Limited (CKPCL, a general construction and infrastructure development company publicly listed on the Thai Stock Exchange); twenty-five percent owned by Natee Synergy (an investment holding company that is a wholly-owned subsidiary of Global Power Synergy Company Limited, itself a wholly owned subsidiary of PTT Public Company Limited, an outcome of the privatization of the Petroleum Authority of Thailand, the latter now listed on the Thai Stock Exchange, but in which the Thai Government retains the largest shareholding); thirteen percent owned by EGCO (a publicly listed company on the Thai Stock Exchange incorporated by EGAT and in which EGAT

---

226   Johns, supra note 156, p. 360.
227   *Location*, Xayaburi Power Company Limited, http://www.xayaburi.com/Location_eng.aspx, accessed July 19, 2016.
228   Background Material on Pöyry's Assignment, supra note 225, p. 8.
229   See Ashwini Chitnis, 'The Xayaburi Power Purchase Agreement: An Independent Review,' *International Rivers* (2013), p. 8, https://www.internationalrivers.org/sites/default/files/attached-files/xayaburi_dam_ppa_analysis_final_report_2013.pdf, accessed July 19, 2016.
230   Background Material on Pöyry's Assignment, supra note 225, p. 8.
231   'Feasibility Study: Xayaburi Hydroelectric Power Project,' *Ch. Karnchang Public Company Limited* (2010).

retains a shareholding of approximately twenty-five percent); seven percent owned by Bangkok Expressway (a company listed on the Thai Stock Exchange); and five percent owned by P.T. Construction and Irrigation Company Limited (a Lao-based company).[232]

Xayaburi is projected to cost US$3.8 billion and will be funded with approximately 71% debt and 29% equity. The debt financing amounts to approximately 88 billion Thai baht in syndicated loans from five Thai private commercial banks (Bangkok Bank, Kasikorn Bank, Krung Thai Bank, Siam Commercial Bank, and TISCO Bank) and a loan guarantee from the Thai Exim Bank.[233]

Considering that Xayaburi is located on the Mekong River mainstream, it is subject to an additional process of 'prior inter-governmental consultation' pursuant to Article 5 of the 1995 Mekong Agreement.[234] This stands in contrast to NT2, which needed only to provide prior notification to the other MRC parties. Prior consultation is defined by the 1995 Mekong Agreement as:

> Timely notification plus additional data and information to the Joint Committee as provided in the Rules for Water Utilization and Inter-Basin Diversion under Article 26, that would allow the other member riparians to discuss and evaluate the impact of the proposed use upon their uses of water and any other affects, which is the basis for arriving at an agreement. Prior consultation is neither a right to veto the use nor unilateral right to use water by any riparian without taking into account other riparians' rights.[235]

As discussed in Part D above, the PNPCA and associated guidelines were concluded by the MRC parties to govern the parameters of the consultation process. The PNPCA process was put into operation for the first time, in September 2010, when the Government of Lao PDR gave formal notice to the MRC Joint Committee of its proposal to proceed with the Xayaburi project's development.[236]

---

232   Johns, supra note 156, p. 361.
233   Ibid.
234   1995 Mekong Agreement, supra note 116.
235   Ibid.
236   Mekong River Commission Secretariat, 'Proposed Xayaburi Dam Project—Mekong River: Prior Consultation Project Review Report,' *Mekong River Commission* (2011), p. i, http://www.mrcmekong.org/assets/Publications/Reports/PC-Proj-Review-Report-Xaiyaburi-24-3-11.pdf, accessed July 19, 2016.

Arguably the PNPCA process largely failed to reconcile the competing differences between the parties, and several measures to improve the process have been proposed to address issues that arose in the Xayaburi PNPCA.[237] In 2014, the Australian government (a provider of funding to assist with the implementation of the PNPCA) summarized the observations of analysts from whom it had commissioned a review of this process as follows:

> The *formal process* for the Xayaburi PNPCA has involved submission of documents, working group meetings, national consultations, deliberations by the MRC Joint Committee and finally a decision by the MRC Council ... The *total process* has been more complicated and has also included bilateral discussions, the launching and subsequent debate catalyzed by the mainstream dams Strategic Environmental Assessment, extensive lobbying by developers and concerned scientists, the Save the Mekong Campaign, film-making and media reporting.[238]

The consultation process conducted, as part of both the PNPCA implementation and the monitoring architecture otherwise installed around Xayaburi, differed from its NT2 corollary. For example, consultations were convened in Cambodia, Thailand, and Viet Nam regarding Xayaburi, but no similar public consultation has yet been conducted within Lao PDR.[239]

After reviewing the MRC prior consultation report, Viet Nam, Cambodia, and Thailand continued to hold strong concerns in several areas regarding gaps in the technical knowledge and studies of the project, the predicted impact on the environment and livelihoods of the Basin's population, and the need for wider consultations.[240] Because the parties could not agree on a way forward, Xayaburi was tabled for consideration at the ministerial level. The Lao PDR government hired Pöyry, a Finnish-based consulting firm, to assess the project's compliance with the MRC requirements. Pöyry indicated the requirements were met, and the Lao authorities gave the green light to Ch. Karnchang

---

237 See Alistair Rieu-Clarke,'Notification and Consultation Procedures Under the Mekong Agreement: Insights from the Xayaburi Controversy,' *Asian Journal of International Law*, Vol. 5(1), pp. 143–175 (2015).
238 Julia Niblett, 'Letter from Julia Niblett, Australian Government Department of Foreign Affairs and Trade to Pianporn Deetes, Thailand Campaign Coordinator, International Rivers,' *International Rivers* (2014), http://www.internationalrivers.org/files/attached-files/responseausaid.pdf, accessed July 19, 2016.
239 Johns, supra note 156, p. 363.
240 Rieu-Clarke, supra note 238, p. 153.

and the dam construction went ahead unilaterally in the face of protest of the downstream neighbours.[241]

Construction of Xayaburi continues and is expected to be completed in 2019 in accordance with the initial prediction. According to the Director-General of the Energy Business Department of the Lao government, as of January 2012, Xayaburi was one of ten hydropower projects under construction in Lao PDR with private financing.[242] Two further hydroelectric projects proposed for the Mekong mainstem have also triggered the MRC PNPCA process, including the US$300 million 260 MW Don Sahong Dam (in 2014)[243] and the 912 MW Pak Beng Dam (in 2017).[244]

H   Concluding Remarks

Analysis and concluding thoughts on the lessons learned from the NT2 project can be viewed as a prism through which PPPs in a transboundary international waters context may be critically reviewed, improved and strengthened. There are 260 international watercourses, encompassing over 45% of the surface of the earth, are relied upon by over 40% of the world's population and account for over 80% of global river flows. International watercourses are 'essential to produce food, power industry, quench our thirst and support ecosystems.'[245] To fully realize these benefits, oftentimes significant infrastructure investment is necessary. PPPs present an attractive, and perhaps only, option to fund certain large infrastructure projects for many countries. However, PPPs must balance the imperative of the private sector to derive a healthy return on investment with the public need to obtain a cost-effective product that meets its desired specifications. Governments need to consider the potential social and environmental impacts that PPP projects on international watercourses

---

241   Ibid.
242   Johns, supra note 156, p. 364.
243   *Don Sahong Hydropower Project*, Mekong River Commission, http://www.mrcmekong.org/topics/pnpca-prior-consultation/don-sahong-hydropower-project/, accessed January 13, 2017.
244   'Official Prior Consultation of the Pak Beng Hydropower Project Kicked Off,' *Mekong River Commission*, (January 13, 2017), http://www.mrcmekong.org/news-and-events/news/official-prior-consultation-process-of-the-pak-beng-hydropower-project-kicked-off/, accessed January 13, 2017.
245   *International Waters*, Global Environmental Facility, https://www.thegef.org/topics/international-waters, accessed January 13, 2017.

might have on riparian states, and provide adequate information so that these states may study and assess them as well.

PPPs can take many forms, and their effectiveness will be significantly influenced by the interests, capacity, and motivations of the partners involved, as well as the relationships between them. As has been discussed throughout this monograph, the outcome of the NT2 PPP is largely a result of the involvement of the World Bank as a leading partner. The safeguard policies of the Bank, along with several other MDBs, ensured that NT2 did not cause unacceptable environmental and social impacts, and respected the rights of its downstream riparians under international law. Considering the critical role that political risk guarantees played in attracting private sector finance, the government had to accept the stringent conditions and social and environmental programmes of the MDBs.

NT2 serves as a valuable PPP learning model, in part because of the extensive work that the World Bank has done in making their monitoring and evaluation of this project accessible through publicly-available reports.[246] A significant aspect of the World Bank's role as a partner in NT2 was that they encouraged the project to broaden its scope from being just a large-scale dam and hydropower project using Lao PDR resources, to encompass larger goals such as economic growth, social development, creating more reliable energy sources, reducing poverty, strengthening government capacity, and promoting policy reform.[247] The World Bank sought commitments from the Lao PDR government to use revenues from the sale of hydropower to reduce poverty and provide effective environmental and social protection. The World Bank also placed significant financial management requirements on the government and applied safeguard policies in an effort to ensure that construction and operation of the NT2 would not adversely affect the Lao people.[248]

While some critics of NT2 worried that the proposed measures did not go far enough to protect affected people and the surrounding environment, any assessment of the actual socio-environmental impacts of the NT2 goes beyond the scope of this monograph. The World Bank has acknowledged the challenges in applying environmental and social safeguards to NT2, which it attempted to address through the Environmental Assessment and Management Plan,

---

246 *Nam Theun 2 Social and Environmental Project*, World Bank Group, http://projects.worldbank.org/P049290/nam-theun-2-social-environment-project?lang=en&tab=overview, accessed December 11, 2016; see in particular Porter & Shivakumar, supra note 69.
247 Porter & Shivakumar, supra note 69, p. 129.
248 Ibid., p. 130.

the Social Development Plan, and the Social and Environment Management Framework and First Operational Plan.[249]

Key learning points from their experience in addressing these concerns in the NT2 context have been noted. In particular, the World Bank found that establishing credibility with mainstream NGOs and initiating an early dialogue with government on issues of 'corruption, equitable treatment of those affected by the project, transparent and accountable use of revenues, and provision of social services' were crucial.[250] The consequences of not raising such issues at an early stage can be significant, including causing costly delays and increased uncertainty for developers, not to mention the potential impact on the people and environment of the region if these obstacles cannot be overcome. The NT2 has opened up new potential for the involvement of powerful partners such as the World Bank to positively influence the direction and impact of massive infrastructure projects, which are well-known to have significant effects on local populations and environments.

The experience of the successful implementation of NT2 provided the Lao PDR government with a strong precedent to show the private sector that it could be trusted as a locale for investing their funds in large PPP infrastructure projects. As a result, the political risk guarantees that were involved with NT2 were not needed to convince various Thai banks to invest in the Xayaburi project, which subsequently proceeded without the involvement of MDBs as sources of funding, guarantors of private sector investment, and guidance influence throughout the project. Without the strict conditions that were imposed by these MDBs for their involvement, it is notable that the Xayaburi project appears to have created much more significant controversy regarding its environmental and social impacts, both domestically and with respect to its downstream neighbours. This appears to have created a difficult challenge for the MRC to overcome to ensure that the MRC remains an effective forum for the cooperative management of the Mekong River's resources.

One potential area for future research is the assessment of the differences in socio-environmental impacts between the NT2 and the Xayaburi Dams to gain a better understanding of the real impacts of the World Bank's safeguard policies in such settings. This could be particularly informative for the Lao PDR government, as plans for new hydropower dams on the mainstream of the Mekong River are currently underway despite lingering concerns about

---

249   Ibid., p. 134.
250   Ibid., pp. 139–140.

damage to wild fisheries and a rice bowl delta that supports 60 million people in the region.[251]

The countries sharing the Lancang-Mekong River are entering a new era of hydropolitics with a growing number of hydropower dams throughout the basin. Three 'powersheds,' conceptualized as physical, institutional, and political constructs that connect dams to major power markets in China, Thailand and Vietnam, are transforming the nature–society relations of the watershed.[252] In the process, new conditions are produced within which the region's hydropolitics unfold.[253] This is epitomized by the 'Lancang-Mekong Cooperation' framework, a new initiative led by China that proposes programmes on both economic and water resource development, and anticipates hydrodiplomacy via China's dam-engineered control of the headwaters.[254] These are interesting times for the Mekong River Basin.

List of References

About MRC, Mekong River Commission, http://www.mrcmekong.org/about-mrc/.

Agreement on the Cooperation for the Sustainable Development of the Mekong River Basin, 5 April 1995, Kingdom of Cambodia, Lao People's Democratic Republic, Kingdom of Thailand, and the Socialist Republic of Viet Nam, http://www.mrcmekong.org/assets/Publications/policies/agreement-Apr95.pdf.

Alexander, Nancy, *The Age of Megaprojects*, Project Syndicate (July 10, 2015), http://www.project-syndicate.org/commentary/g20-infrastructure-investment-by-nancy-alexander-2015-07.

Aquastat: Mekong Basin, Food and Agriculture Organization of the United Nations (2011), http://www.fao.org/nr/water/aquastat/basins/mekong/index.stm.

Armstrong, Scott C., 'Water is for Fighting: Transnational Legal Disputes in the Mekong River Basin,' *Vermont Journal of Environmental Law*, Vol. 17(1), pp. 1–26 (2015).

---

251 'Laos Proceeds with Third Contentious Mekong Dam,' *The Irrawaddy* (November 8, 2016), http://www.irrawaddy.com/news/asia/laos-proceeds-with-third-contentious-mekong-dam.html, accessed December 11, 2016.

252 Carl Middleton & Jeremy Allouche, 'Watershed or Powershed? Critical Hydropolitics, China and the "Lancang-Mekong Cooperation Framework",' *The International Spectator*, Vol. 51(3), pp. 100–117 (2016), DOI: 10.1080/03932729.2016.1209385, p. 100.

253 Ibid.

254 Ibid.

'Asian Infrastructure Investment Bank Environmental and Social Framework,' *The Asian Infrastructure Investment Bank* (2016), http://www.aiib.org/uploadfile/2016/0226/20160226043633542.pdf.

Backer, Ellen, 'The Mekong River Commission: Does it work, and how does the Mekong Basin's geography influence its effectiveness?,' *Südostasien Aktuell*, Vol. 26(4) (2007), pp. 31–55.

'Background Material on Pöyry's Assignment,' *Pöyry* (2012), http://www.poyry.com/sites/default/files/imce/eng_xayaburi_hpp_09112012_final.pdf.

Badissy, Mohammed et al., 'Understanding Power Purchase Agreements,' Vol.1.3, *United States Department of Commerce—Commercial Law Development Program* (2014), http://cldp.doc.gov/sites/default/files/Understanding_Power_Purchase_Agreements.pdf.

Browder, Greg, '*Negotiating an International Regime for Water Allocation in the Mekong River Basin*' (Unpublished PhD dissertation, Stanford University, 1998).

Cai, Jin-Yong, 'A Letter from IFC executive vice president and chief executive officer Jin-Yong Cai,' *International Finance Corporation, World Bank Group* (2015), http://www.ifc.org/wps/wcm/connect/corp_ext_content/ifc_external_corporate_site/annual+report+2015/2015+online+report/leadership+perspectives/ar15_jyc+letter.

Case concerning the Gabčíkovo-Nagymaros Project (Hungary v. Slovakia), Judgment of 25 September 1997, [1997] ICJ Rep 7.

Chitnis, Ashwini, 'The Xayaburi Power Purchase Agreement: An Independent Review,' *International Rivers* (2013), https://www.internationalrivers.org/sites/default/files/attached-files/xayaburi_dam_ppa_analysis_final_report_2013.pdf.

'CK Gets B19bn environmental contracts for Xayaburi Dam,' *Bangkok Post* (May 18, 2016), http://www.bangkokpost.com/news/asean/978185/ck-gets-b19bn-environmental-contract-for-xayaburi-dam.

Colverson, Samuel, & Oshani Perera, 'Harnessing the Power of Public-Private Partnerships: The Role of Hybrid Financing Strategies in Sustainable Development,' *International Institute for Sustainable Development* (2012), http://www.iisd.org/pdf/2012/harnessing_ppp.pdf.

Colverson, Samuel, & Oshani Perera, 'Sustainable Development: Is There a Role for Public-Private Partnerships?,' *International Institute for Sustainable Development* (2011), http://www.iisd.org/pdf/2011/sust_markets_PB_PPP.pdf.

Concessions, Build-Operate-Transfer (BOT) and Design-Build-Operate (DBO) Projects, World Bank Group, Public-Private-Partnership in Infrastructure Resource Center, http://ppp.worldbank.org/public-private-partnership/agreements/concessions-bots-dbos.

'Construction Forges Ahead at Xayaburi Dam,' *Bangkok Post* (July 22, 2012), http://www.pressreader.com/thailand/bangkok-post/20120722/281479273536819.

Corfu Channel (United Kingdom v. Albania), [1949] ICJ Rep 4.

Development Partners & Partner Organisations, Mekong River Commission, http://www.mrcmekong.org/about-mrc/development-partners-and-partner-organisations/.

Don Sahong Hydropower Project, Mekong River Commission, http://www.mrcmekong.org/topics/pnpca-prior-consultation/don-sahong-hydropower-project/.

Environmental and Social Performance Standards and Guidance Notes, International Finance Corporation, World Bank Group, http://www.ifc.org/wps/wcm/connect/topics_ext_content/ifc_external_corporate_site/ifc+sustainability/our+approach/risk+management/performance+standards/environmental+and+social+performance+standards+and+guidance+notes.

'Environmental and Social Practices Handbook,' Version 9.0, *European Investment Bank, Environment, Climate & Social Office Projects Directorate* (2013), http://www.eib.org/attachments/strategies/environmental_and_social_practices_handbook_en.pdf.

European PPP Expertise Center (EPEC), European Investment Bank, http://www.eib.org/epec/index.htm.

'Feasibility Study: Xayaburi Hydroelectric Power Project,' *Ch. Karnchang Public Company Limited* (2010).

'Financial Statements and Independent Auditors' Report Year ended 31 December 2014,' *Mekong River Commission* (2015), http://www.mrcmekong.org/assets/Publications/governance/Part-II-MRC-FS-Audit-2014-FINAL.pdf.

Fisher, Jonah, 'Laos Approves Xayaburi 'Mega' Dam on Mekong,' *British Broadcasting Corporation* (November 6, 2012), http://www.bbc.com/news/world-asia-20203072.

Foreign Direct Investment, Net Inflows (BOP, current US$), World Bank Group, http://data.worldbank.org/indicator/BX.KLT.DINV.CD.WD?display=graph&locations=LA.

Gies, Erica, 'A Dam Revival, Despite Risks,' *The New York Times* (November 19, 2014), http://www.nytimes.com/2014/11/20/business/energy-environment/private-funding-brings-a-boom-in-hydropower-with-high-costs.html?_r=1.

Goichot, Marc, 'Multiple Dams are an Ominous Threat to Life on the Mekong River,' *The Guardian* (May 6, 2015), https://www.theguardian.com/sustainable-business/2015/may/06/dams-hydropower-mekong-river-thailand-laos-don-sahong-xayaburi.

'Guidebook on Promoting Good Governance in Public-Private Partnerships,' *United Nations Economic Commission for Europe* (2008), http://www.unece.org/fileadmin/DAM/ceci/publications/ppp.pdf.

Guidelines on Implementation of the Procedures for Notification, Prior Consultation and Agreement, August 31, 2005, Kingdom of Cambodia, Lao People's Democratic Republic, Kingdom of Thailand, and the Socialist Republic of Viet Nam, http://www.mrcmekong.org/assets/Publications/policies/Guidelines-on-implementation-of-the-PNPCA.pdf.

Guislain, Pierre, 'The Privitization Challenge—A Strategic, Legal, and Institutional Analysis of International Experience,' *The World Bank* (1997), http://documents.worldbank.org/curated/en/138121468739240495/The-privatization-challenge-a-strategic-legal-and-institutional-analysis-of-international-experience.

History, Mekong River Commission, http://www.mrcmekong.org/about-mrc/history/.

Hydrology, Mekong River Commission, http://www.mrcmekong.org/mekong-basin/hydrology/.

'Hydropower in Asia: The Nam Theun 2 Project,' *World Bank Group, Multilateral Investment Guarantee Agency* (2006), https://www.miga.org/documents/NT206.pdf.

Indus Waters Kishenganga Arbitration (Pakistan v. India) (Partial Award) (Permanent Court of Arbitration, February 18, 2013), https://pcacases.com/web/sendAttach/1681.

International Centre for Environmental Management (ICEM), 'Strategic Environmental Assessment of Hydropower on the Mekong Mainstream: Summary of the Final Report,' *ICEM* (2010), http://www.mrcmekong.org/assets/Publications/Consultations/SEA-Hydropower/SEA-FR-summary-13oct.pdf.

International Rivers, 'The New Great Walls: a Guide to China's Oversea Dam Industry,' Second Edition, *International Rivers* (2012), https://www.internationalrivers.org/sites/default/files/attached-files/intlrivers_newgreatwalls_2012_2.pdf.

International Waters, Global Environmental Facility, https://www.thegef.org/topics/international-waters.

Johns, Fleur, 'On Failing Forward: Neoliberal Legality in the Mekong River Basin,' *Cornell International Law Journal*, Vol. 48(2) (2015), pp. 347–383, http://www.lawschool.cornell.edu/research/ILJ/upload/Johns-fnal.pdf.

Ke, Jian, & Qi Gao, 'Only One Mekong: Developing Transboundary EIA Proceedures of Mekong River Basin,' *Pace Environmental Law Review*, Vol. 30(3) (2013), pp. 950–1004, http://digitalcommons.pace.edu/pelr/vol30/iss3/3.

Key Features of Common Law or Civil Law Systems, World Bank Group, Public-Private-Partnership in Infrastructure Resource Center, http://ppp.worldbank.org/public-private-partnership/legislation-regulation/framework-assessment/legal-systems/common-vs-civil-law.

Kim, Jim Yong, 'Tackling the Most Difficult Problems: Infrastructure, Ebola and Climate Change,' *World Bank Group* (October 10, 2014), http://www.worldbank.org/en/news/speech/2014/10/10/speech-world-bank-group-president-jim-yong-kim-tackling-difficult-problems-infrastructure-ebola-climate-change.

Kuenzer, Claudia, et al., 'Understanding the Impact of Hydropower Developments in the Context of Upstream-Downstream Relations in the Mekong River Basin,' *Sustainability Science*, Vol. 8(4) (2013), pp. 565–584.

Kurlantzick, Joshua, 'In Southeast Asia, Big Dams Raise Big Concerns,' *Council on Foreign Relations* (June 30, 2011), http://blogs.cfr.org/asia/2011/06/30/in-southeast-asia-big-dams-raise-big-concerns/.

Lake Lanoux Arbitration (France v. Spain), 24 I.L.R. 101 (1957).

Lao PDR | Data, World Bank Group (2015), http://data.worldbank.org/country/lao-pdr?display=graph.

Lao PDR Overview, World Bank Group (2016), http://www.worldbank.org/en/country/lao/overview.

'Laos Proceeds with Third Contentious Mekong Dam,' *The Irrawaddy* (November 8, 2016), http://www.irrawaddy.com/news/asia/laos-proceeds-with-third-contentious-mekong-dam.html.

Lawson, Frank, 'Sustainable Development Along International Watercourses: Is Progress Being Made?,' *University of Denver Water Law Review*, Vol. 16(2) (2013), pp. 323–348.

Legal and Regulatory Issues Concerning Public-Private Partnerships, World Bank Group, Public-Private-Partnership in Infrastructure Resource Center, http://ppp.worldbank.org/public-private-partnership/legislation-regulation.

Location, Xayaburi Power Company Limited, http://www.xayaburi.com/Location_eng.aspx.

Magnusson, Tomas, 'Sovereign Financial Guarantees,' Paper prepared for *UNCTAD, UNDP, & UNITAR Workshop on Management of a Debt Office*, Tbilisi, Georgia (April 23, 1999).

Maheandiran, Bernadette, 'Calling for Clarity: How Uncertainty Undermines the Legitimacy of the Dispute Resolution System under the OECD Guidelines for Multinational Enterprises,' *Harvard Negotiation Law Review*, Vol. 20 (2015), pp. 205–244.

Matsukawa, Tomoko, & Odo Habeck, 'Review of Risk Mitigation Instruments for Infrastructure Financing and Recent Trends and Developments,' *Public Private Infrastructure Advisory Facility of the World Bank* (2007), https://openknowledge.worldbank.org/bitstream/handle/10986/6778/405300Risk0mit101OFFICIAL0USE0ONLY1.pdf?sequence=1&isAllowed=y.

McCaffrey, Stephen, 'The Contribution of the UN Convention on the Law of the Non-Navigational Uses of International Watercourses,' *International Journal of Global Environmental Issues*, Vol. 1(3) (2001), pp. 250–263.

McCaffrey, Stephen, *The Law of International Watercourses*, Second Edition, Oxford University Press (2007).

Mekong Integrated Water Resources Management Project, Mekong River Commission, http://www.mrcmekong.org/about-mrc/programmes/mekong-integrated-water-resources-management-project/.

Mekong River Commission Secretariat, 'Proposed Xayaburi Dam Project—Mekong River: Prior Consultation Project Review Report,' *Mekong River Commission* (2011), http://www.mrcmekong.org/assets/Publications/Reports/PC-Proj-Review-Report-Xaiyaburi-24-3-11.pdf.

Middleton, Carl, & Jeremy Allouche, 'Watershed or Powershed? Critical Hydropolitics, China and the "Lancang-Mekong Cooperation Framework",' *The International Spectator*, Vol. 51(3) (2016), pp. 100–117, DOI: 10.1080/03932729.2016.1209385.

Nam Theun 2 Power Company Limited, 'Nam Theun 2 Hydroelectric Project, Summary of the Concession Agreement between The Government of the Lao PDR and Nam Theun 2 Power Company, as of November, 2005,' http://siteresources.worldbank.org/INTLAOPRD/Resources/293582–1092106399982/492430–1092106479653/SummaryofCA.pdf.

Nam Theun 2 Social and Environmental Project, World Bank Group, http://projects.worldbank.org/P049290/nam-theun-2-social-environment-project?lang=en&tab=overview.

Natural Resources, Mekong River Commission, http://www.mrcmekong.org/mekong-basin/natural-resources/.

Niblett, Julia, 'Letter from Julia Niblett, Australian Government Department of Foreign Affairs and Trade to Pianporn Deetes, Thailand Campaign Coordinator, International Rivers,' *International Rivers* (2014), http://www.internationalrivers.org/files/attached-files/responseausaid.pdf.

Nickson, Andrew, & Claudia Vargas, 'The Limitations of Water Regulation: The Failure of the Cochabamba Concession in Bolivia,' *Bulletin of Latin American Research*, Vol. 21(1) (2002), pp. 99–120.

'Official Prior Consultation of the Pak Beng Hydropower Project Kicked Off,' *Mekong River Commission* (January 13, 2017), http://www.mrcmekong.org/news-and-events/news/official-prior-consultation-process-of-the-pak-beng-hydropower-project-kicked-off/.

Öjendal, Joakim, & Kurt Jensen, 'Politics and Development of the Mekong River Basin: Trans-boundary Dilemmas and Participatory Ambitions,' *in* Joakim Öjendal, Stina Hansson, & Sofie Hellberg (eds), *Politics and Development in a Trans-boundary Watershed: The Case of the Lower Mekong Basin*, pp. 37–59, (Springer Netherlands, 2012).

Operational Manual BP 7.50—Projects on International Waterways, World Bank Group (March 2012), https://policies.worldbank.org/sites/ppf3/PPFDocuments/Forms/DispPage.aspx?docid=1843.

Operational Manual OP 4.03, Performance Standards for Private Sector Activities, World Bank Group (2013), https://policies.worldbank.org/sites/ppf3/PPFDocuments/090224b0822f7442.pdf.

Operations Manual, Asian Development Bank, http://www.adb.org/documents/operations-manual.

'Operations Manual: Bank Policies,' *Asian Development Bank* (2013), http://www.adb.org/sites/default/files/institutional-document/31483/om-f1–20131001.pdf.

Organisational Structure, Mekong River Commission, http://www.mrcmekong.org/about-mrc/organisational-structure/.

Our Funding: We raise capital through bond issuances, International Finance Corporation, World Bank Group, http://www.ifc.org/wps/wcm/connect/corp_ext_content/ifc_external_corporate_site/about+ifc_new/ifc+governance/funding/ourfunding.

Paisley, Richard Kyle, Patrick Weiler, & Taylor Henshaw, 'Transboundary International Waters Governance Through the Prism of the Mekong River Basin,' *in* Janice Gray, Cameron Holley, & Rosemary Rayfuse (eds), *Trans-jurisdictional Water Law and Governance*, pp. 43–61 (Earthscan Studies in Water Resource Management Routledge, Taylor & Francis Group, 2016).

Petty, Martin, 'Laos Defies Neighbours on Dam Project—Environmentalists,' *Reuters* (June 23, 2011), http://www.reuters.com/article/laos-dam-idUSL3E7HN1L320110623.

Population growth (annual %), World Bank Group (2015), http://data.worldbank.org/indicator/SP.POP.GROW/countries/LA?display=graph.

Porter, Ian C., & Jayasankar Shivakumar (eds), *Doing a Dam Better: The Lao People's Democratic Republic and the Story of Nam Theun 2* (World Bank, 2011), http://documents.worldbank.org/curated/en/200041468044952974/pdf/584400PUB0ID161Better09780821369852.pdf.

PPP Knowledge Lab—Countries, World Bank Group, Public-Private-Partnership in Infrastructure Resource Center, https://pppknowledgelab.org/countries.

'PPP Knowledge Lab: MDBs' Collaboration Brings You the First-ever Comprehensive Online Resource for Public-Private Partnerships,' *World Bank Group* (January 25, 2016), http://www.worldbank.org/en/news/feature/2016/01/25/ppp-knowledge-lab.

'Private Participation in Infrastructure Database (PPIDB)—Half Year Update (January–June 2016),' *World Bank Group* (2016), https://ppi.worldbank.org/~/media/GIAWB/PPI/Documents/Global-Notes/H1–2016-Global-Update.pdf.

Procedures for Notification, Prior Consultation and Agreement, November 13, 2003, Kingdom of Cambodia, Lao People's Democratic Republic, Kingdom of Thailand, and the Socialist Republic of Viet Nam, http://www.mrcmekong.org/assets/Publications/policies/Procedures-Notification-Prior-Consultation-Agreement.pdf.

Project in Brief, Nam Theun 2 Power Company, http://www.namtheun2.com/index.php/about-us/project-in-brief.

Projects & Operations: Mekong River Water Utilization Project, World Bank Group, http://www.worldbank.org/projects/P045864/mekong-river-water-utilization-project?lang=en.

Public-Private Infrastructure Advisory Facility (PPIAF), World Bank Group, http://www.ppiaf.org.

Public-Private Partnerships, Overview, World Bank Group, http://www.worldbank.org/en/topic/publicprivatepartnerships/overview.

Public-Private-Partnership in Infrastructure Resource Centre (PPPIRC), World Bank Group, https://ppp.worldbank.org/public-private-partnership/.

'Public-Private Partnerships Reference Guide,' V. 2.0, *World Bank Group* (2014), http://www-wds.worldbank.org/external/default/WDSContentServer/WDSP/IB/2014/09/08/000442464_20140908133431/Rendered/PDF/903840PPP0Refe0Box385311B000PUBLIC0.pdf.

'Report on Recommended PPP Contractual Provisions,' 2015 Edition, *World Bank Group* (2015), http://ppp.worldbank.org/public-private-partnership/sites/ppp.worldbank.org/files/ppp_testdumb/documents/150808_wbg_report_on_recommended_ppp_contractual_provisions.pdf.

Review and Update of World Bank Safeguard Policies, World Bank Group, Consultations, https://consultations.worldbank.org/consultation/review-and-update-world-bank-safeguard-policies.

Rieu-Clarke, Alistair, 'Notification and Consultation Procedures Under the Mekong Agreement: Insights from the Xayaburi Controversy,' *Asian Journal of International Law*, Vol. 5(1) (2015), pp. 143–175.

Rodriguez, Federico, 'Annual Report 2014: Mekong River Commission,' *Mekong River Commission* (2015), http://www.mrcmekong.org/assets/Publications/governance/MRC-Annual-Report-2014.pdf.

Rogoff, Kenneth, 'Will China's Infrastructure Bank Work?,' *The Guardian* (April 7, 2015), http://www.theguardian.com/business/2015/apr/07/will-chinas-infrastructure-bank-work.

Rondon, Rodrigo C., '*The Law of Transnational Water Resource Projects: Transnationalism in the Brazilian Water Sector?*,' (JSD Dissertation submitted to the McGeorge School of Law of the University of the Pacific, 2012).

Salman, Salman, & Daniel Bradlow, 'Regulatory Frameworks for Water Resources Management: A Comparative Study,' Law, Justice, and Development Series No. 36216, *World Bank Group* (2006), http://web.worldbank.org/archive/website01021/WEB/IMAGES/36216ORE.PDF.

Salman, Salman, & Laurence Boisson de Chazournes, 'International Water Courses, Enhancing Cooperation and Managing Conflict, Proceedings of a World Bank Seminar,' World Bank Technical Paper No. 414, *World Bank Group* (1998).

Salman, Salman, 'The World Bank Policy for Projects on International Waterways: An Historical and Legal Analysis,' Law, Justice, and Development Series No. 48741, *World Bank Group* (2009), http://documents.worldbank.org/curated/en/276451468325130824/pdf/487410PUB0inte101Official0Use0Only1.pdf.

Sanderson, Henry, & Michael Forsythe, *China's Superbank. Debt, Oil and Influence—How China Development Bank is Rewriting the Rules of Finance* (Wiley-Bloomberg Press, 2013).

Schmeier, Susanne, 'Resilience to Climate Change-Induced Challenges in the Mekong River Basin: The Role of the MRC,' *World Bank Group* (2011), http://documents.worldbank.org/curated/en/630751468330303325/Resilience-to-climate-change-induced-challenges-in-the-Mekong-river-basin-the-role-of-the-MRC.

Shareholders & Financing, Nam Theun 2 Power Company, http://www.namtheun2.com/index.php/about-us/shareholders.

Sinha, Sidharth, 'Nam Theun 2 (NT2) Hydroelectric Project,' *Indian Institute of Management* (2007).

Standardized Agreements, Bidding Documents and Guidance Manuals, World Bank Group, Public-Private-Partnership in Infrastructure Resource Center (2016), http://ppp.worldbank.org/public-private-partnership/standardized-agreements-bidding-documents-and-guidance-manuals#Standardized%20PPP%20Contracts.

'Statement by the Heads of the Multilateral Development Banks and the IMF on Infrastructure,' *World Bank Group* (November 13, 2014), http://www.worldbank.org/en/news/press-release/2014/11/13/statement-heads-multilateral-development-banks-imf-infrastructure.

'Statement on the Release of the NT2 Panel of Experts 24th Report,' *World Bank Group* (November 9, 2015), http://www.worldbank.org/en/news/press-release/2015/11/05/statement-on-the-release-of-the-nt2-panel-of-experts-24th-report.

Stiglitz, Joseph, 'The Post Washington Consensus,' *The Initiative for Policy Dialogue* (2004), http://intldept.uoregon.edu/wp-content/uploads/2015/03/Yarris-Joya-5.1.15-Brown-Bag-Article.pdf.

'Substandard Dam Assessment Opens Way to Fisheries Destruction on Mekong,' *World Wildlife Fund* (April 14, 2011), http://wwf.panda.org/wwf_news/press_releases/?200016/Substandard-dam-assessment-opens-way-to-fisheries-destruction-on-Mekong.

'Sustainability Policy and Guidelines,' *Nordic Investment Bank* (2012), http://www.nib.int/filebank/56-Sustainability_Policy_Guidelines-2012.pdf.

Tan, F., 'Laos' Hydropower Generation Capacity to Jump Almost Four-fold by 2020,' *Daily Mail* (October 28, 2014), http://www.dailymail.co.uk/wires/reuters/article-2810681/Laos-hydropower-generation-capacity-jump-four-fold-2020.html.

Tarlock, Dan, 'Toward a More Robust International Water Law of Cooperation to Address Droughts and Ecosystem Conservation,' *Georgetown Environmental Law Review*, Vol. 28(2) (2016), pp. 261–290.

Technical Information, Nam Theun 2 Power Company, http://www.namtheun2.com/index.php/about-us/techinfo.

'Thai State Agencies Likely to Get Away with Xayaburi Dam Construction,' *Prachatai English* (November 30, 2015), http://www.prachatai.com/english/node/5650.

'The Asian Infrastructure Investment Bank: The Infrastructure Gap,' *The Economist* (March 21, 2015), http://www.economist.com/news/asia/21646740-development-finance-helps-china-win-friends-and-influence-american-allies-infrastructure-gap.

The EPEC PPP Guide, European Investment Bank, European PPP Expertise Center, http://www.eib.org/epec/g2g/index.htm.

'The ISH 0306 Study: Development of Guidelines for Hydropower Environmental Impact Mitigation and Risk Management in the Lower Mekong Mainstream and Tributaries,' *Mekong River Commission* (2015), http://www.mrcmekong.org/assets/Publications/policies/1st-Interim-Report-ISH0306-Volume-1-The-Guidelines-Final.pdf.

'The Mekong River: Lies, Dams and Statistics: Xayaburi and Vientiane,' *The Economist* (April 26, 2012), http://www.economist.com/blogs/banyan/2012/07/mekong-river.

Trail Smelter Arbitration (United States v. Canada), 3 R.I.A.A. 1911, 1965 (1941).

Um, W. et al., 'Report and Recommendation of the President to the Board of Directors on a Proposed Loan to the Lao People's Democratic Republic for the Greater Mekong Subregion: Nam Theun 2 Hydroelectric Project,' *Asian Development Bank* (2005).

UNGA Res 2669 (XXV), UN Doc. A/8202 (December 8, 1970).

Anglo-Iranian Oil Co. (United Kingdom v. Iran), Judgment of 22 July 1952 (Preliminary Objection)[1952] ICJ Rep 2.

United Nations Convention on the Law of the Non-Navigational Uses of International Watercourses, UN Doc. A/RES/51/869 (21 May 1997); 36 *ILM* 700 (1997).

United Nations General Assembly (UNGA), 51st Session, 99th Plenary Meeting, UN Doc. A/51/PV.99 (May 21, 1997).

United Nations, 'Depositary Notification,' C.N.271.2014.TREATIES-XXVII.12, https://treaties.un.org/doc/Publication/CN/2014/CN.271.2014-Eng.pdf.

Update: Nam Theun 2 Hydropower Project, Laos, European Investment Bank, http://www.eib.org/infocentre/press/news/topical_briefs/2005-november-01-nam-theun-2-hydropower-project-laos.htm.

Urban, Frauke et al., 'South-South Technology Transfer of Low-Carbon Innovation: Large Chinese Hydropower Dams in Cambodia,' *Sustainable Development*, Vol. 23(4) (2015), pp. 232–244, http://onlinelibrary.wiley.com/doi/10.1002/sd.1590/full.

Vinson, Sara et al., 'International Environmental Law: The Year in Review,' *American Bar Association*, Vol. 48 (2014), pp. 435–452, http://www.americanbar.org/content/dam/aba/uncategorized/international_law/environmental.authcheckdam.pdf.

Watt, Nicholas, Paul Lewis, & Tania Branigan, 'US Anger at Britain Joining Chinese Led Investment Bank AIIB,' *The Guardian* (March 13, 2015), http://www.theguardian.com/us-news/2015/mar/13/white-house-pointedly-asks-uk-to-use-its-voice-as-part-of-chinese-led-bank.

Wolf, Aaron, & Joshua Newton, 'Case Study Trans-boundary Dispute Resolution: the Mekong Committee,' *Program in Water Conflict Management and Transformation* (2007), http://www.transboundarywaters.orst.edu/research/case_studies/Documents/mekong.pdf.

'World Bank and AIIB sign First Co-Financing Framework Agreement,' *World Bank Group* (April 13, 2016), http://www.worldbank.org/en/news/press-release/2016/04/13/world-bank-and-aiib-sign-first-co-financing-framework-agreement.

'World Bank Board Approves New Environmental and Social Framework,' *World Bank Group* (August 4, 2016), http://www.worldbank.org/en/news/press-release/2016/08/04/world-bank-board-approves-new-environmental-and-social-framework.

'World Bank Performance Standards for Private Sector Activities, Guidance Note,' *World Bank Group*, http://siteresources.worldbank.org/EXTSAFEPOL/Resources/OPBP4.03GNApr22Webclean.pdf?resourceurlname=OPBP4.03GNApr22Webclean.pdf.

'World Bank Environmental and Social Framework: Setting Environmental and Social Standards for Investment Project Financing,' *World Bank Group* (August 4, 2016), https://consultations.worldbank.org/Data/hub/files/consultation-template/review-and-update-world-bank-safeguard-policies/en/materials/the_esf_clean_final_for_public_disclosure_post_board_august_4.pdf.

Wright, Christopher, & Alexis, Rwabizambuga, 'Institutional pressures, corporate reputation, and voluntary codes of conduct: An examination of the equator principles,' *Business and Society Review*, Vol. 111(1) (2006), pp. 89–117.

'Xayaburi Dam Building Pact Signed,' *Eco-Business* (April 17, 2012), http://www.eco-business.com/news/xayaburi-dam-building-pact-signed/.

Xayaburi Hydroelectric Power Project, Ch. Karnchang Public Company Limited, http://www.ch-karnchang.co.th/en/#/project/detail/112/energy-xayaburi-hydroelectric-power-project.

Xayaburi Power Company Limited: Private Company Information, Bloomberg, http://www.bloomberg.com/research/stocks/private/snapshot.asp?privcapid=113025177.

Printed in the United States
By Bookmasters